THE

DOWNFALL OF PREMPEH

BY THE SAME AUTHOR

PIGSTICKING
CAVALRY INSTRUCTION
RECONNAISSANCE AND SCOUTING

Frontispiece SEIZURE OF THE PALACE, KUMASSI *Page 128*

THE
DOWNFALL OF PREMPEH

A DIARY OF LIFE WITH THE NATIVE LEVY IN ASHANTI
1895–96

By Major R. S. S. BADEN-POWELL
13TH HUSSARS
COMMANDING THE NATIVE LEVY

WITH A CHAPTER ON THE POLITICAL AND
COMMERCIAL POSITION OF ASHANTI

BY

Sir GEORGE BADEN-POWELL, K.C.M.G., M.P.

SECOND EDITION

The Naval & Military Press Ltd

Published by

The Naval & Military Press Ltd
Unit 5 Riverside, Brambleside,
Bellbrook Industrial Estate,
Uckfield, East Sussex,
TN22 1QQ England

Tel: +44 (0) 1825 749494
Fax: +44 (0) 1825 765701

www.naval-military-press.com
www.nmarchive.com

In reprinting in facsimile from the original, any imperfections are inevitably reproduced and the quality may fall short of modern type and cartographic standards.

DEDICATED

(WITHOUT HIS PERMISSION)

TO

CHIEF ANDOH OF ELMINA

MY GUIDE, ADVISER

AND FRIEND

CONTENTS

		PAGE
I.	REASONS FOR THE ASHANTI EXPEDITION OF 1895-96	15
II.	PRELIMINARIES TO THE EXPEDITION	36
III.	LOCAL PREPARATIONS	45
IV.	AT CAPE COAST CASTLE	53
V.	THE LEVY STARTS	55
VI.	IN THE BUSH	59
VII.	PIONEER WORK	68
VIII.	THE SCOUTS	84
IX.	THE BEKWAI COLUMN	90
X.	FORWARD MOVEMENTS	106
XI.	IN KUMASSI	110
XII.	PREPARING THE "COUP"	119
XIII.	THE DOWNFALL	123
XIV.	AFTER EVENTS	132
XV.	THE COASTWARD MARCH	139
XVI.	HOMEWARD BOUND	152
XVII.	THE FORMATION OF A NATIVE LEVY	162
	POLICY AND WEALTH IN ASHANTI, 1895	181

LIST OF ILLUSTRATIONS

	PAGE
SEIZURE OF THE PALACE, KUMASSI	*Frontispiece*
SKETCH MAP OF THE MARCH TO KUMASSI	15
KROBOS GATHERING TEETH IN THE SACRIFICIAL GROVE	24
HUMAN SACRIFICE AT BANTAMA	28
PORTRAIT OF KING PREMPEH	30
PRINCE CHRISTIAN VICTOR LANDING	54
LAYING THE FIELD TELEGRAPH IN THE BUSH	64
BIRD'S-EYE VIEW OF PRAHSU	66
CHRISTMAS DINNER IN CAMP	72
PRINCE HENRY IN THE BUSH	80
SCOUTING AT NIGHT	88
SPECIAL SERVICE CORPS ON THE MARCH	92
HOISTING THE FLAG AT BEKWAI	100
BIRD'S-EYE VIEW OF KUMASSI	110
KING PREMPEH WATCHING THE ARRIVAL OF TROOPS	114
CAPTURE OF ONE OF PREMPEH'S SCOUTS BY THE AUTHOR	120
PALAVER AND SUBMISSION OF KING PREMPEH	124
SUBMISSION OF PREMPEH, JANUARY 20, 1896	126
EMBARKATION OF KING PREMPEH	149
A MINISTERING ANGEL	154
NATIVE LEVY BUILDING A FORT	168
EXAMINING A PRISONER	176

THE AUTHOR'S APOLOGY TO THE READER

ONE lives but to learn.

Whatever may have been the political result of the late expedition on the Gold Coast, its military aim was altogether defeated by the passive submission of the Ashantis.

I am not too proud to take a cue from our late foes. Therefore, in offering these notes to the public, I would at once disarm any intending critics by giving in to everything they may urge against me.

The book does not purport to be a full and detailed history of the operations,—my position with the native levy, at a usual distance of several days' march from the central direction of affairs, precludes the accuracy and personal knowledge necessary for such a task, and I should hope that there will be many historians far better qualified, who will produce the necessary history.

THE AUTHOR'S APOLOGY

My sketch—for it shall be nothing more—will merely be a rough diary of the campaign from my point of view. I have one object, and one only, in writing. That object is, to escape the further importunity of my friends.

On every side I am badgered—and I suppose that most of the other members of the expedition have been similarly badgered—with the remark:

"Oh, you have come back? Now I *do* hope you are writing a book about it. You are wasting your opportunities if you don't."

These importunities have reached a climax. I will take the plunge. I will shut myself up for four days, and will overhaul my diary.

I only beg of the reader not to judge me harshly, but to picture me entering on the fray with a faltering pen, dragged on by over-zealous friends, and bolstered up with the kind assistance of the *Journal of the Royal United Service Institute*, the *Daily Graphic*, the *Daily Chronicle*, and the *Graphic*, whose editors have generously allowed me to draw upon them for material.

That my tale should not be entirely futile, I shall endeavour to make it point a moral, and to save the reader the trouble of wading through its tedious pages. I will here at once say that the moral may be summed up thus:

TO THE READER

A smile and a stick will carry you through any difficulty in the world, more especially if you act upon the old West Coast motto, "Softly, softly, catchee monkey."

This axiom would not have been offered did it not hold good equally in the lesser as in the larger developments of the campaign. The expedition itself, well-disposed, yet determined, was at once a smile and a stick. By quietly taking possession of Ashanti, it has practically acquired the vast Hinterland beyond — it has softly caught the monkey. And the principle is being carried out in all quarters of the world. In Siam, in Venezuela, and up the Nile, England goes softly, softly, catching her monkey.

And what is a sound principle for an empire is a safe one for an individual.

R. S. S. B-P.

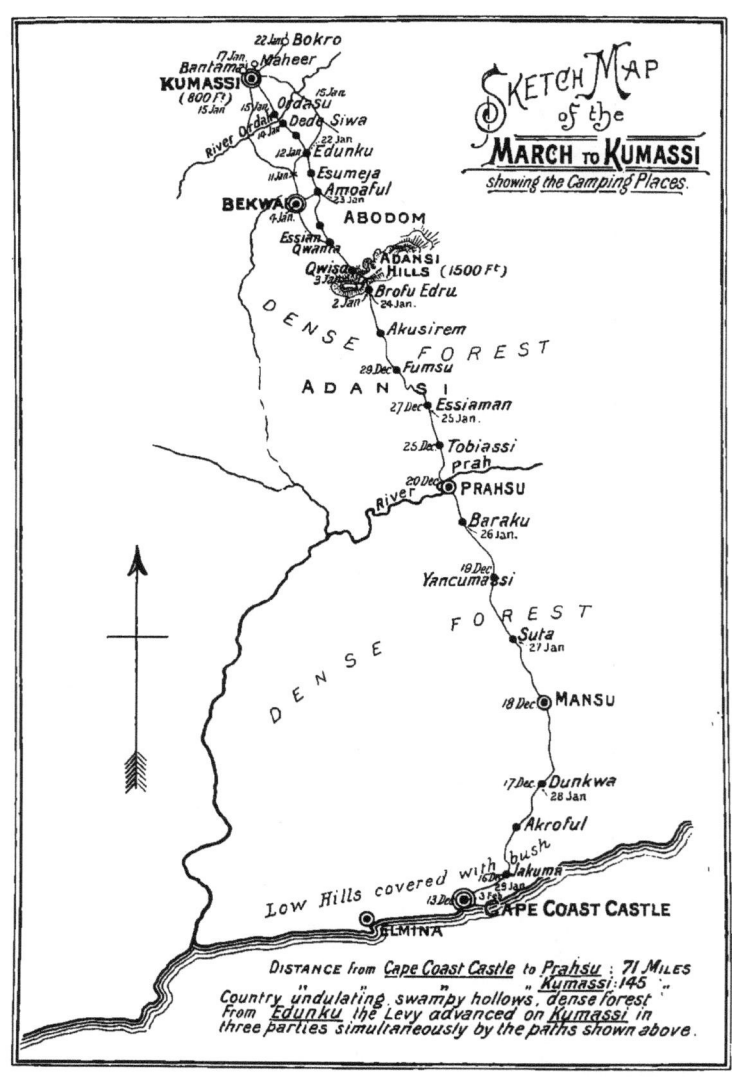

THE DOWNFALL OF PREMPEH

I

REASONS FOR THE ASHANTI EXPEDITION OF 1895–96

In the African bush one may see a lion making his meal on the beast which he unaided has hunted, and has slain by his mighty power; and round him, shrieking and snarling, snatching and tearing, there skips a craven pack of jackals.

One need not go so far as Africa to seek a similar scene. Within a hundred miles of Westminster it may be found.

When a travelling Briton has returned from roaming among the broad lands of our empire beyond the seas, he finds that his ideas have become enlarged, his "bosom swells with pride" at his being an heritor of this vast prize of

THE DOWNFALL OF PREMPEH

generations of British lions, and he realises for the first time what it is "to be an Englishman," and how there is not much temptation "to belong to any other nation"—so long as our navy rules the seas.

But should he feel a little too "uppish" in this elation and pride of birth, he can readily find an antidote. Let him obtain a ticket for the Strangers' Gallery in the House of Commons, and let him go and see for himself the working of what the nation is pleased to call its brain. There he will find—on both sides of the House (for I have no party predilections)—a few lions and a great many jackals behind them. The petty jabber and snarl of these as they snatch and worry at the subject under discussion well-nigh drowns the occasional, meaning "sough" of their betters.

A growl is enough to scatter them all like chaff, but only for a moment, and anon they are back again, blathering as before.

The scene fills one with a sense of humiliation, and yet, on the other hand, it shows the lions in even a better light than before: they have to carry out their hunting not merely unaided, but handicapped by the incessant yapping at their heels of a pack utterly incapable of hunting for itself.

REASONS FOR THE EXPEDITION

To one just back from Ashanti not many days ago, it was particularly pleasing to hear the Secretary of State for the Colonies replying, with reference to that country, to a chorus of yaps. In a brief, but very complete manner, he stated the reasons which had led to the despatch of the expedition under Sir Francis Scott. The main contentions which he had to meet were, firstly, that the claim on the King of Ashanti which produced the expedition was absolutely unjustifiable; and, secondly, that even if it were justifiable, it could have been secured by a means much less costly than an expedition to Kumassi. As a preliminary to dealing with these questions, Mr. Chamberlain disclaimed any ulterior motive in the expedition as having respect to the doings of the French in West Africa—the expedition was undertaken solely in the interests of the Gold Coast Colony, and at the request, often repeated, of the inhabitants of that colony. Both they and the Government considered that steps must be taken to suppress what was neither more nor less than an intolerable and injurious nuisance. The government of the King of Ashanti had, ever since 1874, stood in the way of civilisation, of trade, and of the interests of the people themselves, and should, on these general grounds alone, be put

THE DOWNFALL OF PREMPEH

a stop to. He put it thus: "From the date of the war in 1873 and 1874 this district of Africa, which is, I believe, extremely rich,—certainly rich in natural resources, probably rich in mineral resources,—has been devastated, destroyed, and ruined by inter-tribal disputes, and especially by the evil government of the authorities of Ashanti. No sooner was the present ruler installed as king of the country than he began to make war upon every tribe in the neighbourhood, and the consequent loss of life was very great. I often think it is so extraordinary for gentlemen like the hon. member for Caithness to talk of the loss of life involved in the expedition. It cannot be placed in the same category as the loss of life which has been going on year after year, month after month, simply because we had not the courage and the resolution to make the expedition. (Cheers.) I think the duty of this country in regard to all these savage countries over which we are called upon to exercise some sort of dominion is to establish, at the earliest possible date, *Pax Britannica*, and force these people to keep the peace amongst themselves (cheers), and by so doing, whatever may be the destruction of life in an expedition which brings about this result, it will be nothing if weighed in the balance against

REASONS FOR THE EXPEDITION

the annual loss of life which goes on so long as we keep away. What is the state of things in Ashanti and in many other of these West African and African possessions? The people are not a bad people. The natives are, on the whole, perfectly willing to work, and if they fight, they fight because they cannot help themselves. They would always rather settle down to commercial or agricultural pursuits if they were allowed to do so, but in such cases as that we are considering, the government is so atrociously bad that they are not allowed to do so. No man is safe in the enjoyment of his own property, and as long as that is the case, no one has any inducement to work."

But in addition to these general grounds for action being taken against the Ashanti régime, there exist more particular reasons for it in the refusal of the king to carry out the provisions of the treaty of 1874.

The danger of allowing treaty contracts to be evaded is fairly well understood among European nations, but the results of slackness or leniency in their enforcement are none the less dangerous when the treaty has been made with an uncivilised potentate, since his neighbours are quick to note any sign of weakness or loss of prestige on the part of the white contracting party, and they in

THE DOWNFALL OF PREMPEH

their turn gain courage to make a stand against the white ruler and his claims over them.

In Ashanti the abuse had been allowed to go on far too long. Natives near our border—ay, within it too—had seen year after year go by, and the Ashanti liberty taking the form of licence more and more pronounced, with little or no restraint beyond mild and useless remonstrance on our part. Naturally this raised the Ashantis once more in their estimation, while it lowered our prestige in a corresponding degree; and although the people were sufficiently knowing to see that under our government they were their own masters and were able to carry out any ideas of commerce that they might entertain, still they also saw that, as far as local indications went, the Ashantis were equal in power to the white men, and, as a natural consequence, they were much inclined at least to waver in their allegiance to us.

"Britons never will be slaves," and Britons are so peculiarly imbued with a notion of fair-play that they will not see anybody else in a state of slavery either, if they can prevent it.

Slaves in some parts of the world form the currency of the country; in others they are the beasts of burden and the machinery; often their lot is mercilessly hard, though not always.

REASONS FOR THE EXPEDITION

Wherever there is a good market for them, it is to the interest of the owner to keep them well fed and in good condition. In those parts where domestic slavery prevails, there is often little or no hardship. An occasional lick from a whip is, to an unintelligent savage, but a small matter where in the opposite scale he has the very substantial compensation of protection, food, and home,—advantages which are not always shared by his white brother when fate has frowned and has turned him into the cold to work out his living among the unemployed.

The worst part of slavery is, as a rule, the hardships entailed in the slave-caravan marches, which have to be conducted at a forced pace over desert and devious routes, in order to avoid the good intentions of the European anti-slavery forces.

But in no part of the world does slavery appear to be more detestable than in Ashanti. Slaves, other than those obtained by raids into neighbours' territory, have here to be smuggled through the various "spheres," French, German, and English, which are beginning to hem the country in on every side. The climate they are brought to is a sickly one for men bred up-country.

They are not required for currency, since gold-dust is the medium here.

THE DOWNFALL OF PREMPEH

Nor are they required to any considerable extent as labourers, since the Ashanti lives merely on vegetables, which in this country want little or no cultivation.

And yet there is a strong demand for slaves. They are wanted for human sacrifice. Stop human sacrifice, and you deal a fatal blow to the slave trade, while you render raiding an unprofitable game.

Up till the time of the expedition raiding had been carried on systematically in direct contravention of treaty. "The expedition was necessary also for the protection of other tribes. Every tribe in the neighbourhood of Ashanti lived in terror of its life from the king, who had on several occasions destroyed, one after another, tribes which had sought our protection. There were at least half a dozen separate tribes under separate kings or chieftains who had been driven out of their country and to a large extent destroyed, the whole trade and commerce being utterly ruined in consequence of the continued raids, made against the representations of the British authorities, by the King of Ashanti. In order to prevent that, from time to time the British Government took some of the tribes under its protection. In my opinion a great

REASONS FOR THE EXPEDITION

mistake was made in refusing sooner to take under our protection tribes that asked that protection merely in order that they might engage in peaceful commerce, always with the result that the tribe was immediately afterwards eaten up by the tribes of Ashanti. On one occasion the tribes of Ashanti marched into another kingdom which had been taken under the protection of the British Government. We had to send, at considerable expense, an armed force in order to protect these territories. It is true that in the presence of that force the tribes of the King of Ashanti were withdrawn. But it was only under threat of our intervention that they were withdrawn. The finances of the colony have suffered for years by keeping up larger forces in order to protect tribes under our protection. I think I have said enough to show that we should have been wanting in our duty if we had not insisted that this state of things should be stopped."

In England we scarcely realise the extent to which human sacrifice had been carried on in Ashanti previous to the late expedition, but evidences were not wanting to show it.

In the first place, the name Kumassi means "the death-place."

The town possessed no less than three places

THE DOWNFALL OF PREMPEH

of execution; one, for private executions, was at the palace; a second, for public decapitations, was on the parade-ground; a third, for fetish sacrifices, was in the sacred village of Bantama. Close to the parade-ground was the grove into which the remains of the victims were flung, and which very aptly was known as "Golgotha" to the members of the force. The ground here was found covered with skulls and bones of hundreds of victims. At Bantama was the celebrated execution bowl, which was fully described by Bowdich in his account of Kumassi in 1817. It is a large brass basin some five feet in diameter. It is ornamented with four small lions, and a number of round knobs all round its rim, except at one part, where there is a space for the victim's neck to rest on the edge. The blood of the victims was allowed to putrefy in the bowl, and leaves of certain herbs being added, it was considered a very valuable fetish medicine. The bowl has now been brought to England. Then in Kumassi are two blocks of houses occupied entirely by the executioners—one being assigned to the sacrificial, the other to the criminal executioners. Among the loot taken in the houses of Prempeh and of his chiefs were several "blood stools," or stools which had been used as blocks

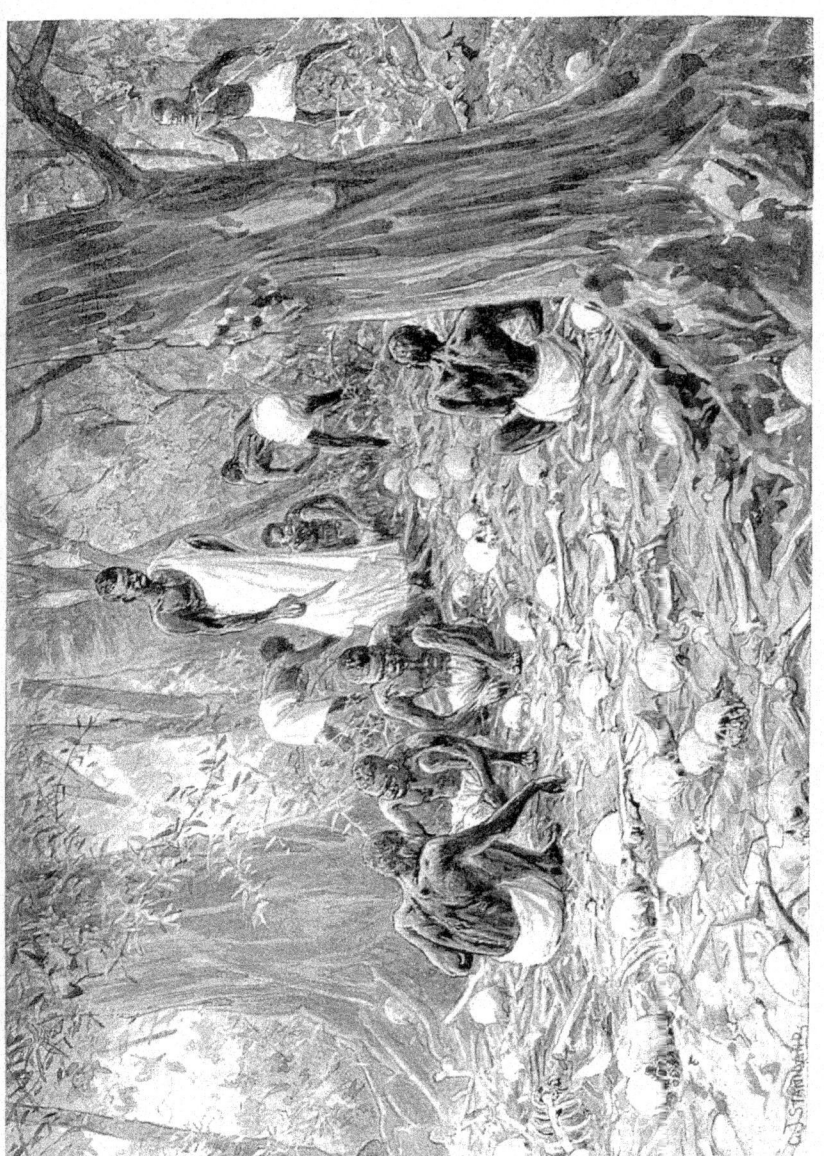

Krobos gathering Teeth in the Sacrificial Grove

REASONS FOR THE EXPEDITION

for executions, and which bore very visible signs of having been so used. In these notes, be it remembered, we are only dealing with Kumassi, but every king—and there were some half a dozen of them in the Ashanti empire—had powers of life and death over his subjects, and carried out his human sacrifices on a minor scale in his own capital.

In fact, the ex-king of Bekwai was deposed on account of his over-indulgence in that form of amusement.

Any great public function was seized on as an excuse for human sacrifices. There was the annual "yam custom," or harvest festival, at which large numbers of victims were often offered to the gods. Then the king went every quarter to pay his devotions to the shades of his ancestors at Bantama, and this demanded the deaths of twenty men over the great bowl on each occasion. On the death of any great personage, two of the household slaves were at once killed on the threshold of the door, in order to attend their master immediately in his new life, and his grave was afterwards lined with the bodies of more slaves who were to form his retinue in the spirit world. It was thought all the better if, during the burial, one of the atten-

THE DOWNFALL OF PREMPEH

dant mourners could be stunned by a club, and dropped, still breathing, into the grave before it was filled in. In the case of a great lady dying, slave-girls were the victims. This custom of sacrifice at funerals was called "washing the grave." On the death of a king the custom of washing the grave involved enormous sacrifices. Then sacrifices were also made to propitiate the gods when war was about to be entered upon, or other trouble was impending. Victims were also killed to deter an enemy from approaching the capital: sometimes they were impaled and set up on the path, with their hand pointing to the enemy and bidding him to retire. At other times the victim was beheaded and the head replaced looking in the wrong direction; or he was buried alive in the pathway, standing upright, with only his head above ground, to remain thus until starvation, or —what was infinitely worse—the ants made an end of him. Then there was a death penalty for the infraction of various laws. For instance, anybody who found a nugget of gold and who did not send it at once to the king was liable to decapitation; so also was anybody who picked up anything of value lying on the parade-ground, or who sat down in the shade of the fetish tree at Bantama. Indeed, if the king desired an execu-

REASONS FOR THE EXPEDITION

tion at any time, he did not look far for an excuse. It is even said that on one occasion he preferred a richer colour in the red stucco on the walls of the palace, and that for this purpose the blood of four hundred virgins was used. I have purposely refrained elsewhere from giving numbers, because, although our informants supplied them, West African natives are notoriously inexact in this respect. The victims of sacrifices were almost always slaves or prisoners of war. Slaves were often sent in to the king in lieu of tribute from his kinglets and chiefs, or as a fine for minor delinquencies. Travelling traders of other tribes, too, were frequently called upon to pay customs dues with a slave or two, and sometimes their own lives were forfeited.

When once a man had been selected and seized for execution, there were only two ways by which he could evade it. One was to repeat the "king's oath"—a certain formula of words—before they could gag him; the other was to break loose from his captors and run as far as the Bantama-Kumassi cross road; if he could reach this point before being overtaken, he was allowed to go free. In order to ensure against their prisoners getting off by either of these methods, the executioners used to spring on the intended

THE DOWNFALL OF PREMPEH

victim from behind, and while one bound his hands behind his back, another drove a knife through both his cheeks, which effectually prevented him from opening his mouth to speak, and in this horrible condition he had to await his turn for execution. When the time came, the executioners, mad with blood, would make a rush for him and force him on to the bowl or stool, whichever served as the block. Then one of them, using a large kind of butcher's knife, would cut into the spine, and so carve the head off. As a rule, the victims were killed without extra torture, but if the order was given for an addition of this kind, the executioners vied with each other in devising original and fiendish forms of suffering. At great executions torture was apparently resorted to in order to please the spectators. It certainly seems that the people had by frequent indulgence become imbued with a kind of blood-lust, and that to them an execution was as attractive an entertainment as is a bull-fight to a Spaniard or a football match to an Englishman.

This custom is one which a clause in the treaty of 1874 stipulated was to cease, but the contract was never carried out by the king. In spite of his promises, sacrifices went on up till the time of the expedition. It was even said that an execu-

HUMAN SACRIFICE AT BANTAMA.

REASONS FOR THE EXPEDITION

tion came off at the palace the day after our arrival in Kumassi.

Another clause of the treaty which King Prempeh had failed to carry into effect was that which promised the maintenance of an open high-road from Kumassi to Cape Coast Castle. The idea of this road was not only to render communication with Kumassi comparatively easy, but also to open a way through the two hundred miles of impassable forest which shut off the rich plains of the Hinterland from access to the coast. It was argued, with reason, that if such road were kept open for pack caravans, a big trade would at once be opened up with the interior; but the king neglected to carry out his part of the treaty. The road was allowed to become overgrown again with the rank, thick jungle of the bush, and the slight foot-track to which if dwindled was used by a few small bands to rubber-dealers, but these traded at great risk and for small returns, owing to the heavy dues and peremptory punishments imposed by the Ashantis on traders passing through their country. Remonstrance had no effect. Without an expedition it looked as though the mass of trade awaiting an outlet from the Hinterland would either die off, or would be diverted into neigh-

THE DOWNFALL OF PREMPEH

bouring countries belonging to France and Germany.

Another item in the bill against the king was the payment of the war indemnity for the last expedition. Of this the first two instalments had been paid, but since then not a stiver.

Briefly, then, we may look on the following as the main reasons and objects for the expedition :—

To put an end to human sacrifice.
To put a stop to slave-trading and raiding.
To ensure peace and security for the neighbouring tribes.
To settle the country and protect the development of trade.
To get paid up the balance of the war indemnity.

Experience had shown that it was of no avail to trust to the king carrying out the terms of a treaty, and therefore it was considered necessary to appoint a Resident at Kumassi who would see that the king carried out his engagements.

The king was asked whether he approved of this plan. At first he altogether refused to accept a Resident. Then he sent insulting replies. Another time he sent no reply. And finally, he declined to deal with the governor of the colony, but sent envoys to England.

PORTRAIT OF KING PREMPEH

Page 30

REASONS FOR THE EXPEDITION

The story of this part of the case was thus stated by the Secretary of State for the Colonies: "The king said he had sent his messengers to see the Queen of England and make known his wishes. Lord Ripon sent word to the Governor of the Gold Coast to tell the messengers if they came to England that they would not be received by the Queen or her representatives. He actually forbade their coming to England, although he did not feel justified in preventing them by force. On what grounds did Lord Ripon take this course? He had many grounds. In the first place, that their character was bad; in the second place, that they were representatives of a king who indulged in human sacrifice, and that the representatives of such a potentate were not to be received by the Queen of England (cries of "Oh, oh!"); and, in the third place, that in dealing with these subject tribes under the circumstances which I have detailed, it would be absolutely ruinous to the governor on the spot if, at any moment you chose, you could pass him by and claim to be received directly in London. We place a great responsibility upon the heads of the governors whom we send out to those distant places, and who have to act very often on the spur of the moment; and if we ourselves reduce

THE DOWNFALL OF PREMPEH

their authority in the eyes of these subjects, there would be simply no end to the representations with which we should have to deal in this country, and to the tricks by which these savage rulers would escape from their responsibility. When I came to office the matter came before me, having been already decided by my predecessor. I do not want on that account in the slightest degree to lessen my responsibility. If I had occupied office at the time Lord Ripon did, I should have taken exactly the same course. These persons came to England, and I refused to receive them. Representations were made to me on their behalf by a member of this House; and I said I would be most happy to receive him, but I refused to recognise him as their representative. He did not desire to be recognised as their representative, but wished on his own account to place before me some statements which he had heard from them. Their statement was to the effect that they had credentials from the King of Ashanti; that they had plenipotentiary authority from him to deal with me as the representative of the Government; and, finally, that they were prepared to accept the terms which I informed the gentleman who saw me it was our intention to demand. Well, I told them I accepted their assurances for what they

REASONS FOR THE EXPEDITION

were worth (laughter); but that Her Majesty's Government would not on that account countermand the expedition. It is very easy, of course, to say we should have stopped the expedition; that we would have saved the expenditure and attained the same result. That is a hypothetical statement. I confess I have not the remotest belief that we should have attained the same result, or anything like it. And I think I have some reason for saying that when I had to make my decision, of course, I did not know all the facts, but what I did know was that if the expedition was held back, and if, thereafter, these so-called envoys were repudiated by the King of Ashanti, not only would great expenditure have been incurred for no purpose, but we should have to repeat the expedition at a time when, owing to the difficulties of season and climate, the loss of life would have been very much greater. I thought the risk too great. What justification has come to hand of the action which we took in this matter? In the first place, these so-called envoys had absolutely no authority whatever to make the terms to which they gave their signature; their credentials were forged credentials, the seal of the King of Ashanti was manufactured in London after they came here (laughter); they had

THE DOWNFALL OF PREMPEH

no power whatever to accept the conditions imposed upon them by Her Majesty's Government; and the only authority they had was authority which they themselves had sought to obtain redress from Her Majesty's Government for the grievances of the Ashanti people. And it is perfectly clear that what I feared would have taken place, and that if they had gone back without an expedition, they would have been repudiated, and properly repudiated, by the Ashanti king. Then it is said, 'Why this display of force?' In order to avoid bloodshed. (Cheers.) It is also said that all this might have been done by a small force, and I believe that is true, but it would not have been done without bloodshed. If we had gone there with a small force, we should have tempted the Ashantis to war. Do not let it be supposed that the Ashanti king had no idea of resistance. You will find that he sent an embassy to Samory, who is a powerful chief, inviting him to join in resisting the British attack; and nothing but the sense of his own impotence prevented a collision which must have resulted in a very considerable amount of bloodshed."

Indeed, as it was, the men had all been called out for war, and had the expedition been a little

REASONS FOR THE EXPEDITION

slower in coming upon the scene, it would, without doubt, have met with a determined resistance. The king would not bring his army into the field until he had had the report of his envoys from England. When they arrived at Kumassi, the expedition was close upon their heels. The Ashantis take time to mobilise and to get all the preliminary fetish-eating and oath-swearing completed, and thus, before they were ready, the British troops were already in Kumassi.

The force then present was sufficiently large and powerful to overawe the natives, who were assembled, be it remembered, under arms, in the villages round about Kumassi; and it was able to effect the arrest of Prempeh, together with the whole of his leading chiefs, at one swoop.

Had a smaller force, or one composed entirely of Houssas and West Indians, attempted a similar *coup*, there is not the slightest doubt that bloodshed, and very probably disaster, would have resulted. In a word, there could not, by any possibility, have been a clearer vindication of the policy of sending a compact force of white troops on this expedition.

II

Preliminaries to the Expedition

14th November 1895.

The pink "flimsy" bearing the magic words, "You are selected to proceed on active service," gives to the recipient a gush of elation such as a flimsy of another kind and of a more tangible value would fail to evoke. From that moment he is a different being. He treads on air, the envy of his non-selected fellow-aspirants. He is like to the happy man who has received a favourable answer to his suit, not only from "her," but, what is more to the point, from her stern parent. He becomes an object of interest to all, and especially to himself. His arrangements for the campaign do not take long. He looks into the sundry packs and parcels that contain his field kit, always ready, and notes deficiencies that have to be made good.

No sooner has his name appeared in the list,

PRELIMINARIES TO EXPEDITION

as published by the press, than circulars flow in upon him from outfitters, money-lenders, insurance agents, and others, anxious to utilise such a chance of sucking money as the occasion may afford. And his daily post is further swelled by letters of congratulation from his friends both far and near. Envious comrades congratulate him, while they beg his help to get them taken too, and ill-spelt appeals come from his men for him to get them to the front. At the War Office he finds that bustle without fussiness prevails, but the number of officers seeking their orders there is far outnumbered by those who have come to beg for any vacancy that may occur.

And then he has to face a medical examination by a board of doctors, who test his soundness in wind and limb and eyes; the dentist sets him up for faring on "hard tack," and the surgeon vaccinates him, as the Gold Coast now teems with smallpox. At stores and shops he spends much time in choosing what he wants from endless stocks of what he is pressed to take. The dealer's estimate of what is necessary differs in a wonderful degree from that which is the outcome of experience. Kind friends press on him presents of varied utility, from hip-baths to tea-coseys. On

THE DOWNFALL OF PREMPEH

every hand he is asked—as though the fact of his being appointed to the expedition made him *ipso facto* a full-blown authority on it—what is to be the actual good of the campaign, apart from the active employment it may give to eager officers and men. And where does the return come in for the expenditure of thousands of pounds and many lives on a bit of West African swamp that can be of no use to anybody?

So he turns to the handbooks and returns of the United Service Institute, and there he finds that this Gold Coast colony produces an annual revenue of some £202,000; its expenses run to something under £180,000; it has an export and import trade of over £720,000 each, of which some £530,000 goes to the United Kingdom; and that the amounts are steadily increasing year by year. But all this trade is only derived from the eastern and western extremities of the country; the trade of the centre remains stagnated and barred by the opposition of one tribe there located, namely, the Ashantis. Were these people to act in a friendly and peaceful manner towards their neighbours, a large increase in the prosperity of all would result; but now, as of old, they remain an obstacle to progress and development. In early times the Phœnicians, and in later times the

PRELIMINARIES TO EXPEDITION

Portuguese, had exploited the riches of the Gold Coast. So long ago as 1366 French traders from Rouen settled there for the purpose of digging gold, and styled their port La Mina (Elmina). These remained there for nigh a hundred years. Danes, Dutch, and English, Portuguese and Swedes soon followed them with trading ventures all along the coast. In 1672 the English Royal African Company established itself at Cape Coast Castle, as well as at several other points, and paid its way till 1821, when, damaged by the abolition of the slave trade, it transferred its property to the Crown.

Meanwhile, the Ashantis had already made themselves unpleasantly known as the bully tribe of that region by their raids on their more feeble neighbours, especially the Fantis of the coast. These latter had come to be considered as the *protégés* of the English. Consequently, after two such raids, in 1807 and 1817, the English established a Resident at Kumassi, but he had to be withdrawn after a short residence, and again the Ashantis came down in 1819. In 1823 they proceeded to invade the Wassaw territory, but the Gold Coast was now a colony of the Crown; the Governor, Sir Charles Macarthy, with 500 native troops and twelve European officers, endeavoured

THE DOWNFALL OF PREMPEH

to oppose their advance. He had, however, committed the usual British fault of under-estimating the strength of his enemy; ammunition ran out (it is even said that through one of those mistakes that do sometimes occur, the kegs which had laboriously been carried to the front as bearing ammunition were found when opened to contain but supplies of vermicelli)—the result—disaster. The Governor's head went to make a drinking-goblet for the savage king, and very few survivors lived to tell the tale. The Ashantis' further advance was only stayed by a deadly outbreak of small-pox in their ranks, so that for a season they withdrew. But two years later again they took the field, this time to find us with our allies well prepared and organised. The result was a very decided victory in our favour, which brought about a lengthened spell of peace and prosperity to the colony. In 1831, Governor Maclean concluded an important treaty with the Ashantis, Fantis, and other tribes, in which the Ashantis renounced their pretended suzerainty over all others, while the Fantis on their part agreed to abstain from giving cause of offence and retributory raids, and all consented to refer to British arbitration any disputes that might arise. To this treaty a further clause was added in 1848, in which Governor

PRELIMINARIES TO EXPEDITION

Winniett obtained the abolition of human sacrifices by the Ashantis.

But the Ashantis were not made for peace or treaties. Blood and loot had for them charms that could not be resisted. In spite of treaties, human sacrifice at the rate of some 3000 per per annum still went on. Raids were attempted in 1853 and 1863. Then, in 1872, the Fantis provoked attack from their ever-ready neighbours by quarrelling with a tribe of Ashanti allies at Elmina. Fighting took place. The British were dragged into it partly to defend their Protectorate and maintain treaties, and partly because the Ashantis had seized and held as prisoners certain Europeans.

Experience had then shown that the natives never felt bound to any extent by treaties, however solemnly they might have been entered upon, and that any show of hesitation, or even of leniency, on the part of the British was construed by friends and foes alike as a sure sign of weakness. Consequently, the expedition under Sir Garnet Wolseley was organised on a footing such as precluded all chance of failure. His main column of 1400 white troops advanced direct on Kumassi, while columns of native allies made demonstrations to divert the Ashanti forces. The

THE DOWNFALL OF PREMPEH

king, recognising our determined front, sent in message after message of submission and promise of amendment in the future; but Sir Garnet took them for what they were worth, and never paused in his onward march; and it was only after the pseudo-submission had been broken down in a series of toughly-contested bush fights that he finally captured and destroyed the capital, and left the king a fugitive.

In the treaty of peace which thereupon resulted, the Ashantis promised to renounce all suzerain rights over various neighbouring tribes, to open their country to trade, to stop human sacrifice, to pay a war indemnity of 50,000 ounces of gold, and to keep the road from Kumassi to the Prah open and clear of bush. And how have these promises been observed? The Ashantis have raided their neighbours, have taken over 2000 Koranzas, traders cannot pass through Ashanti, the main road has never been kept clear of bush, the war indemnity still remains to be paid, and human sacrifice continues as before—to wit, some 2000 captured Koranzas are said to have been decapitated in the past two years, as many as 400 being killed at one time on a special occasion.

As for the expedition itself, matters are being now organised on the most practical and economi-

PRELIMINARIES TO EXPEDITION

cal basis. A picked and compact force is being sent out, consisting of some 2000 regular troops in all. By the time they arrive on the Gold Coast, the staff sent on in advance will have prepared the road before them for the first 70 out of the 120 miles to Coomassie. Five depot camps will have been established between Cape Coast Castle, the base, and the river Prah, which forms the frontier. Bridges will have been built over the numerous rivers and streams, telegraphic communication will have been set up all along the line, and two fortified posts will have been made beyond the Prah to cover the cutting of the road and to protect communications in the enemy's country. Twelve thousand carriers will have been collected for transport of supplies, baggage, and sick. So that our troops will, on arrival, have nothing to do but to march straight forward on to the enemy's capital at the best pace the climate will allow. Already to the northward officers are organising the Koranzas to threaten the Ashanti rear, while native troops are getting into position on his eastward flank. One of the highest authorities in the land has prophesied that the Ashantis will make a stand, and come into action with us about January 9, near Edunku. What wonder, then, that he who has his orders

THE DOWNFALL OF PREMPEH

for the front presses on his final arrangements with a feverish haste, and will only be happy when, one fine morn, he stands upon the deck, with pyjamas blowing in the land breeze, to receive the snaky welcome of the misty, low-lying shore?

III

LOCAL PREPARATIONS

8th December 1895.

M'LALA-PAHNSI, or "the man who lies down to shoot," is the name by which a Zulu describes the man who lays his plans carefully and with full completeness before he embarks on his enterprise. It is the name which such Zulu, were he here, would apply to Sir Francis Scott. Every point that can be foreseen as requiring attention in the present expedition is being provided for. Critics may say that to get everything cut-and-dried beforehand is to dig for oneself a groove that will hold one when a change of circumstances may require a corresponding change of action. But it does not follow that when you have selected your line in the run, you may not change it if the fox alters his course. Moreover, it must by these critics be remembered that in the present enterprise we have not merely one, but two

THE DOWNFALL OF PREMPEH

enemies opposed to us. One is King Prempeh, the other, and more formidable, King Fever. It is against this latter, as much as against the former, that the plans are being laid. His tactics are well known and unvarying, and are therefore to be met with equally regular forethinking.

On arrival at Grand Canary on the 1st inst., Sir Francis found little news awaiting him beyond the disappointing fact that his advance party, owing to stress of weather, was now but four days ahead of him instead of at least a week. The threatened extra delay will probably be got over by extra exertion on the part of all concerned; but extra exertion is above all things to be avoided in the Coast climate if sustained working power is to be maintained. The main duties of the advance party and of the officers already on the spot are—

1. To enrol carriers.
2. To prepare road stations.

In order duly to appreciate the great importance of these two services, it is necessary to consider the nature of the road from Cape Coast Castle to Kumassi.

In the first place, the so-called road is merely a

LOCAL PREPARATIONS

narrow pathway—the best part of it, from Cape Coast to the Prah, is only sufficiently wide for two men moving abreast; beyond the river it has yet to be cleared. It leads for the greater part of its 150 miles through heavy primeval forest. The thick foliage of the trees, interlaced high overhead, causes a deep, dank gloom, through which the sun seldom penetrates. The path winds among the tree stems and bush, now through mud and morass, now over steep ascent or deep ravine. The heavy dews and mists that come with night are laden with malaria for men, while the tsetse fly and horse-sickness infest the forest, and bar it as a death-trap to all beasts of burden.

To plunge a force of white troops at once into this forest, to set them to march and fight and bivouac in the usual way, would be to lay them low at one stroke with sickness. For the first 70 miles of its course, from Cape Coast Castle to the Prah river, the road lies in our own territory, and it is this portion which is now being fully prepared beforehand for the ultimate rapid and unhindered advance of the British troops when they arrive a fortnight or three weeks later. Since baggage animals cannot be employed owing to the "fly" and absence of forage, and Decau-

THE DOWNFALL OF PREMPEH

ville or other mechanical means of transport are impossible by reason of the nature of the ground, it is necessary to use the ordinary system of the country, namely, porters.

For mere regimental transport, that is, conveyance of men's kits, regimental ammunition, sick, etc., the number has to be computed at one carrier per head, which will entail close upon 2000 of them. In addition to these, an army of porters will be required for transport of ordnance, commissariat, hospital, engineer, and other stores. Large supplies and reserve stores of ammunition, arms, food, not only for the fighting men, but also for the host of carriers themselves, stretchers for sick, medicines, telegraph and bridge-making equipment, and a hundred other necessary items, have all to be moved up beforehand to the ultimate base, at the Prah, at Prahsu.

For the whole of this work, then, it is estimated that some 10,000 or 12,000 carriers will be required. The work of collecting these men will in itself be no small task; for although there is not the drain on the local manhood that there was in the last campaign, to serve as armed levies, yet their natural laziness, timidity, and general disregard of their engagements, make it extremely difficult to get them even to come to

LOCAL PREPARATIONS

the scratch. In fact, it is only possible by means of bribes and rewards to the various chiefs — awarded in proportion to the number of men supplied. Then, when they have been assembled and registered, there is a great deal to be done in organising them into proper gangs under responsible men, and in assigning the gangs to their various duties under white officers, and in providing for their punctual rationing and payment, and for their discipline and sanitation.

All this has to be done before the stores can be moved from the landing-place at Cape Coast Castle. Then the limit of work of which a carrier is capable is to carry a 50-lb. load for ten miles, with one day's rest in every five. The relay posts will, therefore, be established at every ten miles, and will include standing camps for the reception of the troops as they march up. But these stations have all to be prepared, bush being cleared, huts erected, water supply perfected, fuel collected, and rations and supplies stored before they can be pronounced ready for use; and furthermore, the advanced base at Prahsu has to be completed with all the bulk of supplies necessary for carrying the troops on beyond the Prah up to Kumassi and back. This means the

THE DOWNFALL OF PREMPEH

transport of hundreds of tons over 70 miles of narrow bush path in 50-lb. packages. To help matters, the path has to be "corduroyed" over bogs, 200 bridges built, and telegraph set up. Then the standing camps, to be effective for preserving the health of the men, have to be prepared in a very thorough manner. Huts are built with wattled walls and palm-thatched roofs, 60 ft. long by 20 ft. wide, with a raised platform along each side to serve as a bed. These will accommodate fifty men each. Eight of such huts, together with others for officers, hospital and supply stores, will constitute a station. Of these stations there will be seven between the coast and Prahsu, near the following points :— Jakuma, Akroful, Dunkwa, Mansu, Suta, Assin Yankummassi, Baracu.

Huts are essential to the health of the troops, as the only protection against the ordinary heavy dews of night and the frequent thunderstorms and tornadoes that sweep over this region. And although thus sheltered overhead, it is of equal importance that the men be protected against the natural poisonous exhalations of the ground ; and the best means to this end is the provision of bed-places standing at least two feet above the floor level. Plenty of fuel is to be provided at each

LOCAL PREPARATIONS

station, not only for cooking purposes, but also for drying the air inside the huts. The supply of abundance of good filtered water forms another important item in the preparation of each station. The comfort and well-being of the men, healthy as well as sick, is being catered for in a most thorough manner, even down to the daily supply of fresh oranges and bananas. Camp police have to be organised to ensure the due observance by the large detachments of carriers of the orders regarding sanitation and discipline laid down for them. Thus it will be seen that there is much to be done before troops need, or should be, landed. Lying idle at the coast while waiting for the road to be completed would inevitably lay them low with fever. Pushing forward before the suplies and camps are ready, would equally mean unnecessary hardships and consequent sickness. And with so very small a force every man is wanted for the fray, especially if Samory, with his mounted braves, should try to pass our flank in the open valley of the Volta. The Ashantis will not move away; our target is a fixed one, and in preparing to shoot at it we should be mad to fire before we have got into the best position for doing so. As our chief is acting on this principle, we may hope, with all con-

THE DOWNFALL OF PREMPEH

fidence, that there will in this case be no repetition of the French campaign in Madagascar — an instance of a fine expedition nearly wrecked by want of sufficient forethought and preparation.

IV

AT CAPE COAST CASTLE

13th December.

AT last we have arrived at the end of our three weeks' voyage, and Cape Coast Castle has shown itself to our longing eyes much as the books describe it. A large, rambling, whitewashed fort standing on a group of rocks on the surf-washed beach. Behind it lies the dull red native town of earthen flat-roofed houses, interspersed with whitewashed bungalows of merchants, and all around the town there rise a mass of small, steep, wooded hills, two or three of which are topped with buildings.

Great open surf-boats take us to the shore, each propelled by a dozen lusty paddlers, sitting sideways on the gunwale, and timing well the dipping of their three-pronged blades with choruses which at times are quite harmonious. Then, as we near the seething beach, a rush of naked helpers runs

THE DOWNFALL OF PREMPEH

the boat well up, and we are landed dry-shod at the castle water-gate. Within the courtyard, with its galleries all round, the bustle and the noise are almost overpowering, as gangs of carriers, both male and female, bring the loads of stores just landed from the ship, to be checked and stored for further use. Perhaps nowhere will you find a more well-trodden grave than that of L. E. L., the poetess, who lies beneath the flags of this same courtyard.

Here, too, are crowds of natives being enrolled and told off into gangs as carriers, to form the chain of depôts that have to be made in anticipation of the arrival of the troops.

SIR FRANCIS SCOTT AND PRINCE CHRISTIAN VICTOR LANDING IN A SURF BOAT

V

THE LEVY STARTS

14th December.

PREPARATIONS such as those I have described take some doing, as they have to be completed before the white troops can usefully be landed; and they have to be pushed on well into the proximity of the enemy. For this reason they demand the presence of a covering force to protect their progress. A small body of Houssas is already engaged on this duty near Prahsu. (Houssas, I may explain, are disciplined native troops drawn from the fighting Mohammedan tribes of the Gold Coast Hinterland, and commanded by white officers; they do not call themselves either "Hoos-as" or "Hussars," but "Howsers.")

An order has now been given that an additional force, composed of native warriors, shall be organised and pushed up to act as covering force in front of the expedition.

THE DOWNFALL OF PREMPEH

It falls to my lot to get together and organise this corps. Fortunately I have the advantage of the valuable assistance of Captain Graham, D.S.O., 5th Lancers, whose other name is "The Sutler." If this implies that he is as business-like as he is enterprising, the title is not inappropriate. One hundred of the Adansi tribe have already been collected and armed by the civil authorities, and have taken up their position as outposts beyond the Prah, in the country from which they have lately been driven by the aggression of the Ashantis.

In addition to these we are to get the services of men of various tribes living nearer to the coast within the colony. Numbers of them are promised by the various kings and chiefs, who, however, on the slightest pretext go back on their engagements with most annoying promptness. At last, after three days' of alternate cajoling and threatening, we get these chiefs to undertake to produce 500 men on the 16th December by noon.

16th December, Noon.

The parade-ground outside the castle lies an arid desert in the midday sun, and the sea-breeze wanders where it listeth. Not a man is there. It is a matter then for a hammock-ride

THE LEVY STARTS

through the slums of the slum that forms the town. Kings are forked out of the hovels where they are lodging, at the end of a stick; they in their turn rouse out their captains, and by two o'clock the army is assembled. Then it is a sight for the gods to see "The Sutler" putting each man in his place. The stupid inertness of the puzzled negro is duller than that of an ox; a dog would grasp your meaning in one-half the time. Men and brothers! They may be brothers, but they certainly are not men.

If it were not for the depressing heat and the urgency of the work, one could sit down and laugh to tears at the absurdity of the thing, but under the circumstances it *is* a little "wearing." But our motto is the old West Coast proverb, "Softly, softly, catchee monkey"; in other words, "Don't flurry; patience gains the day." It was in joke suggested as a maxim for our levy of softly-sneaking scouts, but we came to adopt it as our guiding principle, and I do not believe that a man acting on any other principle could organise a native levy on the West Coast—and live.

Gradually out of chaos order comes. Kings and chiefs are installed as officers, and the men are roughly divided into companies under their orders.

THE DOWNFALL OF PREMPEH

Then the uniform is issued. This consists of nothing more than a red fez for each man, but it gives as much satisfaction to the naked warrior as does his first tunic to the young hussar.

Arms are to be issued to the corps at Prahsu, and that the intervening seventy miles may not be traversed uselessly, each man is now supplied with a commissariat load to carry on his head. At three o'clock the levy is ready for the march.

His Excellency the Governor inspects the ranks, and says a few encouraging words to the leading chiefs and captains. Among the men we muster a few with drums and others who are artists on the horn. The horn in this case consists of a hollowed elephant's tusk, garnished with many human jaw-bones—its notes are never more than two, and those of doleful tone; but at the signal for the march these horns give out a raucous din which, deepened by the rumble of the elephant-hide drums, imparts a martial ardour to the men, and soon the jabbering, laughing mob goes shambling through the streets, bound for the bush beyond.

VI

IN THE BUSH

PRAHSU, 21*st December.*

ON the road at last—from Cape Coast to, or at any rate towards, Kumassi. For the first few miles after we have cleared the bazaar of Cape Coast Castle, the road, a hard gravel path, runs through a labyrinth of small bush-covered hills; but although there is very little sun to-day, the heat is very great, and one is fain to give up one's first resolution of doing all the march on foot in favour of an occasional, if not a frequent, lift in the hammock. The hammock as a conveyance, once you have become accustomed to its motion, and have fitted its hang to suit your taste, is said to be luxurious. Personally I prefer to walk, except where a lift may serve to keep one's feet from wet or head from sun. The hammock itself is a common string one, with a cross-bar affixed to each end. The cross-bar rests

THE DOWNFALL OF PREMPEH

on the heads of the bearers. Over all a light canvas roof is fixed, which serves to keep off the worst of sun or rain from the occupant. The four bearers shamble along at a good pace, balancing the concern on their heads, and can carry one for long distances by day or night without stumble or false steps. The drawback to this method of travel, is that the springiness of the motion forbids all reading or writing that might otherwise usefully occupy many of the hours spent on the march.

But so far as it has gone,—some five days between Prahsu and Cape Coast Castle,—the journey has in no way palled upon us. About fifteen miles from the coast the bush gradually grew in height and density, until the huge bare shafts of the cotton-trees began to tower here and there among the palms, giant ferns, and smaller trees that formed the general mass of foliage. Then we gradually came into regular forest scenery, from which we shall not again emerge till our campaign is over. This same scenery, we were told, would appal us with its deadly dulness, and the depression of the forest would affect our minds most powerfully. Possibly our minds are not sufficiently prehensile to catch the morbid sensation that was promised, and in all

IN THE BUSH

the wondrous woodland that has charmed our eye at every step, the only inharmonious quality that has struck us is its aroma. Yes, walking down the solemn shady aisles of forest giants, whose upper parts gleam far above the dense undergrowth in white pillars against the grey-blue sky, or passing from a sunlit glade into the deep dark crypt of massive bamboo clumps,—places that have aptly been compared with the scenery of the depths of the ocean,—everywhere there hangs the noisome scent that meets you near old cabbage-plots in England. The rule here seems to be, the prettier the spot, the more deadly is its air. Where you see the brilliant red wax-flowers gleaming beneath the great angle-buttresses of a cotton tree, whose stem is covered for 50 feet with ferns and orchids, till 150 feet of creeper, hanging in one dense curtain, meets them from the upper branches, you stand a moment to wonder and admire, when, faugh! the loathsome smell assails and drives you forward. In all the forest scarce a bird or living thing is seen. An occasional robin's song is heard, or the tuneful wail of the "finger-glass bird," while at night the whistle of the crickets and the roar of frogs is broken by the dismal child-like shriek of the sloth.

The path is now narrowed down, and being

THE DOWNFALL OF PREMPEH

almost all in shade, is far more cool for walking than at the outset of the journey—in width about four yards, but often by overgrowth reduced to one. On either side, the dense mass of fern and bush and tangled creeper set in swampy ground prevents all moving off the path. And thus our pace is checked as we find the road in front blocked with a slow-moving mass of loaded carriers—hundreds upon hundreds of them, all working along in gangs, with loads upon their heads of about 50 lbs. apiece. Each gang works under its own chief, and is distinguished by armlets of a certain colour, each armlet bearing the classifying letter and number of the wearer. Here we find yellow armlets carrying cases of "bully" beef; then come grey ones with lime-juice; soon after we find white ones carrying tarred rope for the bridge over the Prah; and then a "lady-pack," with blue and white policemen's armlets, carrying biscuit cases, many a one of them with an additional load in the shape of a brown nodding little baby on her back. The whole of this mass of usually blundering natives was working just like clockwork all along the line within three days of its organisation in the hands of Colonel Ward and his never-tiring staff. Not a load gets lost or

IN THE BUSH

even delayed, not a man is in arrears of his daily pay.

Every three or four miles one passes through a native village—generally a single street of some twenty or thirty houses. Each house consists, as a rule, of three or four small huts or sheds, facing inwards, and forming a little courtyard. These huts are on built-up platforms, with hard mud walls, and roofs thatched with palm-leaves, and their front steps faced with a smooth red-coloured cement. They are kept fairly clean, so that we generally occupied one for our half-way breakfast, or on occasion to sleep the night. In the centre of each village is a tree with seats round it, formed of untrimmed logs, on which the elders of the village sit and smoke and gravely talk. As one leaves the village and plunges once more into the bush, one passes the village fetish ground, well marked by rags and stones and broken pots, all offered as propitiation to the presiding demon of the place. Deep in the bush behind the huts one sees the giant leaves of the plantain groves that yield the staple food of the inhabitants. At every village as we pass we interview the headman on the subject of his crop, and warn him that a daily market must be open for the sale of yams and plantains to our host of carriers; and

THE DOWNFALL OF PREMPEH

though he looks a knowing and a high-class kind of man when strutting forth in his toga-like garment, we find it hard to make him grasp the full meaning of our demand. The brains of these Ashantis are assuredly most non-receptive.

At nearly every ten miles we come upon a rest-camp, in a more or less completed condition, for occupation by the British troops when they come marching up. With no little labour, bush has been cleared away for many hundred yards, and huts have been built up of bamboo frames, with trellis sides and palm-thatched roofs. Within them tables, seats, and bed-places have been made again of split bamboos — accommodation sufficient for some three hundred men, with complement of officers. Store-sheds are being quickly filled with food and ammunition for the force. A.S.C. officers in *déshabillé*, and steaming, are hard at work from dawn till dusk. And then, as far at least as Mansu, half-way to the Prah, the telegraph runs near the path, but taking a more direct line through the bush by a track recently cut out with much and heavy labour. After Mansu the "fetish cord," as the natives call it, no longer hangs on poles, but lies along the ground close to the path. It is the mere field cable of the Engineers that now takes the place of the

LAYING THE FIELD TELEGRAPH IN THE BUSH

IN THE BUSH

more permanent line; and as we press forward, we at length overtake Captain Curtis, R.E., working himself, like his men, half-stripped, and laying out his line at the phenomenal rate of two and a half miles an hour. This in itself is a record that would be hard to beat when all the difficulties of country, climate, and circumstances are taken into consideration.

Here and there along the road we come to bridges over streams and causeways over swamps, all in course of construction at the hands of scores of natives, working with an amount of energy that is most surprising when one sees how few and far between are the ever-travelling, hard-worked white superintendents. Here we meet one gaunt and yellow. Surely we have seen that eye and brow before, although the beard and solar topee do much to disguise the man. His necktie of faded "Old Carthusian" colours makes suspicion a certainty, and once again old schoolfellows are flung together for an hour to talk in an African swamp of old times on English playing-fields. Again we press on through the never-ending dark green aisles, until at length, one sweltering afternoon, we tramp in a melting state — although in the airiest of costumes — into the village camp of

THE DOWNFALL OF PREMPEH

Prahsu. Prahsu is our advanced base on the river Prah.

The big yellow river slowly slides along between its forest-clad banks, and on a low, reed-grown spit the camping-ground is cleared and huts are being built. One double-storeyed house exists, the headquarters of the post, where Major Gordon reigns supreme. A company of Houssas —the war-loving native armed police—is quartered here; a base hospital and base supply and ordnance stores are being made. There is an accumulation of barrels waiting for the rope with which the pontoon bridge is to be constructed.

As we arrive at Prahsu, rumours there are of encounters between our scouts and those of the enemy, and of blood drawn on both sides. We are told that King Prempeh laughs to scorn the proposal that he shall come down to meet the Governor in conference. "The King of the Ashantis is the lord of heaven and of earth." This is an Ashanti proverb up to which the king and his captains are said to be ready to act. To-day, too, we hear that the best Ashanti scouts are now out and about Bekwai to watch our doings, and that the Ashanti plan of campaign is to draw on our force, and then to cut in in rear of it. At anyrate, they seem inclined to fight. That they

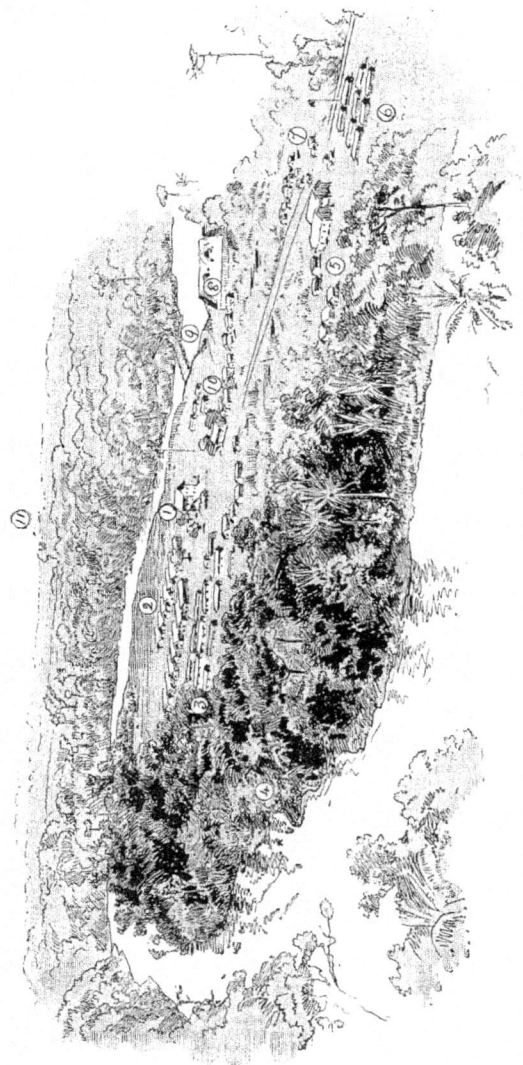

BIRD'S-EYE VIEW OF PRAHSU

1. Commandant's House. 2. British Troops' Company Line. 3. Houses and Lines. 4. Cemetery and Magazine. 5. Hospital. 6. Major Baden-Powell's Regiment. 7. The Village. 8. Supply and Ordnance Stores. 9. River Prah and Pontoon Bridge. 10. Officers' Huts and Lines. 11. Ashanti.

IN THE BUSH

will do so is the great hope of those who toil through the long hot hours in this steaming fetid atmosphere. Nor can one well grudge them the feeling. Of the little band of eight white men now preparing matters in Prahsu, even as I write, three are down with fever. Still they peg away, one day down, the next up and smiling again—but sometimes the smile is a little wan. All that buoys them up is hope—hope that through their "bucking up" their side will win the game.

VII

PIONEER WORK

PRAHSU, *22nd December*.

WHEN one speaks of the boundary between Ashanti and Cape Coast Colony, one's ideas picture the Prah as the natural mark of the border, whereas the actual boundary lies much farther north, beyond the Adansi Hills. Historically and politically, and for most practical purposes, the Prah remains the boundary all the same. The Adansis, who used to inhabit the British portion beyond it—and so formed a buffer tribe between the Ashantis and the colony—have been removed to more eligible quarters in the south, and the district remains a No Man's Land, and practically a bush desert. For the purposes of the expedition the camp at Prahsu, on the bank of the Prah, is a half-way house to Kumassi—comparatively safe from attacks of the enemy by reason of its position at the end of a good road from the coast,

PIONEER WORK

and in a land of plentiful supplies. It is as much the frontier and advanced base to-day as it was in 1874, when it was actually on the border of the enemy's country.

An immense depôt of supplies has now been formed here, and when the forward move commences, no doubt a further advanced base will be formed at the Adansi Hills, thirty-five miles farther on. The supply of stores will be pushed up there for the maintenance of the troops within striking distance of Kumassi. The long line of road between Prahsu and the Adansi Hills has, however, to be prepared with a chain of defensive camps, where convoys can defend themselves should the Ashantis endeavour to cut in on our line of communications. This is a very favourite manœuvre of theirs, and constitutes one of their avowed plans of campaign for the present war. Their system is to secretly cut a path for themselves through the bush away from the line of the main road, but parallel to it. When their scouts have warned them that they have well passed the main force or depôt whose destruction they desire, they cut their way to the road, and then lie in ambush for parties endeavouring to pass up or down, or they make a raid on a convoy in camp; thus with a comparatively small body they are enabled to completely cut off their enemy from his base. It is to guard against such tactics that the native levy has now been ordered into the country across the Prah, together with about 150 of the Houssa police. The advanced outposts are formed by our Adansi company, of 100 men. These are posted on the actual border north of the Adansi Hills, and the scouts are watching every move on the part of the Ashantis; for there are moves of Ashantis going on—small ones, it is true, but they are often the grains of dust that tell which way the wind blows. The Adansis being bushmen and hunters by nature, and subjects for many years of oppression at the hands of the Ashantis, have entered on the work of reconnoitring *con amore*; and although they are only armed with flint-lock guns, they show an amount of keenness in their work that is very noticeable in a country where energy or enterprise on the part of the natives is usually so conspicuously absent. Our main body consists of some 300 Krobos under their king Matikoli, and 100 Mumfords, under chief Brew, and a company of Elminas, under the veteran chief Ando. This fine old warrior bears on his breast the medal for the last Ashanti campaign, where he served for some time in Sir Evelyn Wood's Native Levy,

PIONEER WORK

and afterwards as native adviser on the staff of Lord Wolseley.

23rd December.

At Prahsu, after handing over to the Commissariat department the loads which we have brought up for them, we have got to work on the more complete organisation and training of the levy. After begging and borrowing (sometimes even stealing) any tools of any kind whatsoever, we have started the levy to work in clearing the bush, in building huts, in road-making, and in other useful pioneering work. And in addition to this we are exercising the men at outpost work, and we have issued arms to some of them. But the arms, being very inferior flint-locks,—many of them wanting even the flints,—do not inspire great confidence, and we only hope that ere long a supply of Snider rifles may be issued in their place.

FUMSU, *27th December.*

On the 24th December, after four days usefully, but anxiously, spent at Prahsu, the permission arrived for the levy to cross the Prah, and to continue its advance into the enemy's country. The permission reached us at three

THE DOWNFALL OF PREMPEH

o'clock, and by five the major portion of the levy had been ferried across in the great ferry-boat (a "dugout" hewn from the trunk of an enormous tree, and capable of carrying thirty people). A slight delay was occasioned by one tribe declining to move, but the argument *pro* and *con* did not last long, and eventually we found ourselves practising night-marching up till about nine o'clock, when we reached our camping-ground.

Beyond the Prah we find a very different state of things to that on the southern side. Our road is no longer the comparatively broad, direct, and well-cleared way, but has become a twisty, zigzagging footpath—now clambering over fallen tree-trunks, now twisting through a bog—so narrow and broken as to forbid the use of a hammock for any distance. Villages are very few and very small, and consequently supplies are very scarce for our men and for the carriers of the expedition who are to follow. Road-makers and bush-cutters cannot now be obtained among the native population. Thus the work that falls upon the levy is exceptionally heavy, especially as our supply of tools is somewhat limited, and the natives' idea of using those they have is even more so. Give a man a felling-axe, and he will think it a good weapon for scraping up weeds,

CHRISTMAS DINNER IN CAMP

PIONEER WORK

and a spade he will use for cutting down timber.

Yes, life with a levy, where there are only two of you to work six hundred, might, for a few days, be a diverting experience, if the climate were good and if there were no immediate necessity for the work to be carried to a result. But as things are, it is a pretty powerful exercise, both mental and physical, and by the end of the day one wants but little here below but to drink and to lie down and sleep—or die, you don't care which.

Here is our usual day's routine:—

At early dawn, while the hush of the thick white mist yet hangs above the forest, a pyjama-clad figure creeps from its camp-bed in the palm-leaf hut, and kicks up a sleeping drummer to sound " Reveillé." Then the tall, dark forest wall around the clearing echoes with the boom of the elephant-tusk horns, whose sound is all the more weird since it comes from between the human jaws with which the horns are decorated. The war-drums rumble out a kind of Morse rattle that is quite understandable to its hearers. The men get up readily enough, but it is merely in order to light their fires and to settle down to eat plantains, while the white chiefs take their tubs, quinine, and tea. A further rattling of the drum

THE DOWNFALL OF PREMPEH

for parade produces no result, The king is called for. "Why are your men not on parade?" With a deprecatory smile the king explains that he is suffering from rheumatism in the shoulder, and therefore he, and consequently his tribe, cannot march to-day. He is given a Cockle's pill, and is warned that if he is not ready to march in five minutes, he will be fined a shilling. (The luxury of fining a real, live king to the extent of one shilling!) In five minutes he returns and says that if the white officer will give his men some salt to eat with their "chop" (food), he thinks they will be willing to march.

The white officer grimly says he will get a little salt for them, and proceeds to cut a specimen of a particularly lithe and whippy cane. A hundred pair of eyes are watching him. They read his intention in a moment, and at once there is a stir. A moment later, and *that* portion of the army are off in a long string upon the forward road, with their goods and chattels and chop tied up in bundles on their heads.

But the whole levy is as yet by no means under way. Here a whole company of another tribe is still squatting, eating plantains, and jabbering away, indifferent to every other sound. "Call the chief." Yes, the chief is most willing to do any-

PIONEER WORK

thing; would march straight on to Kumassie if ordered. But his captains are at present engaged in talking over the situation, and he cannot well disturb them. The white chief does not take long about disturbing them, but still the rank and file don't move. The captains have something they would like to communicate to the white chief. "Well, out with it."

The head captain has come to the conclusion, from information received, that the Ashantis are a most cowardly race.

"Quite right. Just what I have told you all along; and if you will only hurry up, we can get right up to them in a few days and smash them."

"Ah! the white chief speaks brave words, but he does not know the ways of the bush warriors. No; the plan which the captains in council have agreed upon is to draw the enemy on by retiring straight away back to Cape Coast Castle. The enemy will follow them, and will run on to the bayonets of the white soldiers who are coming up from the coast."

"A very good plan, but not quite identical with that of the white chief. There is only one plan in his mind, and that is to go forward, and this plan must be carried out by all. He has in his hand a repeating rifle which fires fourteen

THE DOWNFALL OF PREMPEH

shots. When the regiment begins its retirement, he will go to the head of it and will shoot at each man as he comes by. Fourteen corpses will suffice to block up the path. And now any who like to go back on these conditions can do so; the gun is already loaded. Those who like to go forward to get their chop at the next halting-place can move on. Those who like to sit where they are can do so till it is their turn to be tied to a tree, to get a dozen lashes, commencing with this gentleman." Loads are taken up, and in a moment the whole force goes laughing and singing on the forward path.

On through the deep, dark aisles, still foggy with the morning mist and wet with the dripping dew. Twisting and turning, now up, now down, clambering over giant tree-roots or splashing through the sucking mud—all in moist and breathless heat, till, tired and dripping, we reach the next site for a camp. Two hours' rest for midday chop, and then parade. More delays, more excuses, and at last every man has his tool issued to him, and every company has its work assigned to it. No. 1 to clear the bush. No. 2 to cut stockade posts. No. 3 to cut palm-leaf wattle. No. 4 to dig stockade holes. No. 5 to mount sentries and prevent men hiding in huts; and so

PIONEER WORK

on, till every one is at work. We lay out the plan and trace of the fort that is to be built, and of the huts that are to form the camp.

"Hallo! where are the hole-diggers?"

"They have retired to have some chop."

"Chop? they've only just finished two hours of chop."

"Yes—but the white chief works them so hard that they have big appetites."

"They—and you, their chief—will all be fined a day's pay."

"Yes; well, the white man is powerful. Still, we prefer that to not having our chop. Many thanks."

"Oh, but you'll have to work as well. See this little instrument? That's a hunting-crop. Come, I'll show you how it can be used. I'll begin on you, my friend!"

No need to. They all fly to their work. Then you go round. Every company in turn is found sitting down, or eye-serving.

"Down with that tree, my lad—you with the felling-axe! Not know how to use it?"

For three days I felled trees myself, till I found that I could get the tree felled equally well by merely showing the cracker of the hunting-crop. The men had loved to see me work. The

THE DOWNFALL OF PREMPEH

crop came to be called "Volapük," because it was understood by every tribe. But, though often shown, it was never used.

The bush-clearing company are sitting down, not a yard of bush cut. "Why?"

"Oh, we are fishermen by occupation, and don't know anything about bush-cutting."

The bush soon comes down nevertheless, and, what is more wonderful, by sunset there is an open space of some seven or eight acres where this morning there was nothing but a sea of bush jungle. Large palm-thatched sheds have sprung up in regular lines, and in the centre stands a nearly finished fort, with its earth rampart bound up by stockade and wattle. Within it are two huts, for hospital and storehouse. Trains of carriers are already arriving with hundreds of boxes of beef and biscuit to be checked, arranged, and stored. At sunset sounds the drum, the treasure box and ledger are opened, and the command comes up for pay.

"First company—how many men present?"

"Sixty-eight, sir."

"But it has only got fifty-nine on its establishment!"

"Next company."

"All here, sir, but some few men away sick—

PIONEER WORK

and two he never come"—and so on and so on. At last it is over, except that a despatch-runner comes in with a telegram, forwarded from the last telegraph station, to ask from Cape Coast Castle offices immediate reason why the men's pay-list has been sent in in manuscript, instead of on Army Form O 1729!

27th December.

From the advanced scouts to the main body of the expedition is a long step. The antennæ are at Dompoassi, the head and brain are at Prahsu, and the body extends from that place to Cape Coast Castle. The white troops are getting along well now that they are in the bush, but the first march on the coast claimed, alas, two victims to the heat. At Prahsu the headquarters staff are at present concentrated, and occupy a position where they are completely in touch with the whole of the long line of the force, a line a hundred miles in length. The field telegraph is of the greatest value in directing and controlling this immense chain, and has now reached Aku-serim under the energetic arrangements of Captain Curtis. Plenty of work for everybody is the talisman which has so far happily kept the staff in an excellent state of health and energy. Sir

THE DOWNFALL OF PREMPEH

Francis Scott appears the picture of life and freshness. Prince Henry of Battenberg, as military secretary, is in constant attendance on his chief, and shows no sign of feeling the heat. Having allowed his beard to grow, he is now the counterpart of his brother, Prince Louis. He has imported chargers into the country in the shape of a pair of riding donkeys, which are, so far, standing the climate well; but shortly they will have to face the ordeal of the "fly," for about Esiaman, a short distance north of the Prah, the tsetse fly abounds. This little pest,—about the size of a large house-fly,—although to men it is no more harmful than a mosquito, is fatal to a horse or domesticated animal. One bite is said to be sufficient; the system gradually becomes poisoned, and the animal loses strength and dies —all the more rapidly if the weather is wet. Wild animals—probably through generations of inoculation—are proof against the poison, and donkeys are said to be less susceptible to it than other tame beasts. Therefore it is possible that Prince Henry's stud may live to carry him through the campaign. Working hard at his duties as A.D.C., Prince Christian Victor gets through a great amount of work in the day, and, in opposition to Prince Henry, he has shaved

Prince Henry in the Bush

PIONEER WORK

even his moustache. Major Belfield, on whose shoulders the main work of the expedition falls, luckily keeps as well and as energetic as ever was his wont. But there is sickness in the camp, and far too much of it. Three of the medical officers are down with it, and several of the non-commissioned officers and men — especially of the Royal Engineers.

All along the road progress continues. The carriers, thoroughly organised in gangs, are working like clockwork. Tons of supplies are being placed ready in the camps all along the route as far as the Adansi Hills. Over these and beyond, the road is still being cut, and camps being laid out and built. News trickles in daily from the outposts. We now know that Prempeh ordered a council of war last week at Kumassi, and that most of his chiefs attended it, but that several did not, and business was adjourned for their attendance. In the meantime, the envoys who had been to England have returned. The council has again been called, and again one or two chiefs have refrained from attending. The most notable among these absentees is the king of Bekwai, who has a force of some 2000 men, and whose country would be the first to receive the British invasion. He has sent messengers to

THE DOWNFALL OF PREMPEH

Sir Francis Scott expressing his desire to come under British protection. But it is evident that such protection must take an active form, and promptly, for there is little doubt that should Prempeh discover his subject's treason before the British help arrives, the King of Bekwai will lose his head. It is probable, therefore, that a small flying column will be sent with all speed to occupy Bekwai and afford protection to its people. In doing this, such column would also occupy a very strong strategical point on the enemy's flank, which might possibly affect in an important degree the future plans and moves of the Ashantis. Of these there are now collected in Kumassi some 8000 warriors armed with guns and rifles, but apparently not well supplied with ammunition for sustained fighting. The ceremony of taking fetish for war is gradually being carried out—in the leisurely fashion peculiar to all business, however urgent, in this part of the world. Taking fetish is practically the taking, by all the captains and chiefs, of an oath to fight. When all have completed the ceremony, the king gives his assent and his orders for the war.

The system of the army appears to be to sit quietly awaiting the development of affairs, and they protest that they have no intention of

PIONEER WORK

fighting the English. This same protestation they made in 1874, and continued to do so until within a few hours of the battle of Amoaful, so that no reliability can be placed on their statements; and there seems little doubt, from the fact of their being already assembled in arms, that they intend to resist, at anyrate, any attempt to take their capital or their king. But once they have thus satisfied their conscience and established etiquette, they will be only too glad to lay down their arms and to welcome the new order of things. The whole country seems sick and tired of the continual state of war in which they have lived. Over the border they see the people who used to be their slaves now thriving, fat and happy, under the English flag, and they begin to long for something of the kind for themselves. Custom and superstition still partly hold them to the old order, but with very little pressure they will gladly throw that over and accept the new— much to the benefit of themselves and their neighbours.

VIII

THE SCOUTS

DOMPOASSI, 28*th December*.

LEAVING the main body of the native levy at their work of building forts and making roads and camps ready for the advance of the expedition, we come, by a very rapid transition, into another state of things. The road, narrow as it was and broken, now becomes a mere foot track, twisting in and out between the trees, impeded with gnarled roots and boggy ruts. Every now and again a huge fallen tree-trunk blocks the way—sometimes the path goes laboriously round the end of it, at other times one clambers over, and when one has clambered over some four or five of these impediments in the course of a hundred yards, one begins to realise what delay they would cause to a long train of troops on the march. Streams and bogs have to be waded through, being so far

THE SCOUTS

innocent of bridges and of "corduroy." These are points that will be corrected as the levy moves along. Meanwhile, there is a certain pleasure in thus pushing through the bush in its more natural everyday condition. Villages now become very few and far between : mere clusters of huts in forest clearings, containing a population of about a dozen each, all told. Tracks of animals and of hunters become more frequent in the tangled bush. These are tracks that are used by Ashanti scouts, and we notice that our carriers now no longer straggle along the path or spend their voices in loud jabbering, as they have done before the Prah was reached.

At last two figures meet us, quite in keeping with the scene. No clothes beyond a few discoloured rags — their bodies girt about with leathern thongs from which hang powder-gourds and knife-sheaths and bullet-bags of deer's hide. On their shoulders they carry immense long flintlock guns, and round their necks are strings of fetish charms. They come gliding on, laughing, bowing, and shaking hands—these are the first we meet of our scouts. They have heard—goodness knows how—of our arrival, and have come out to meet and escort us on the way. Their

THE DOWNFALL OF PREMPEH

coming to meet us means a little step of ten miles or so over the mountain, but that is as nothing to these fine wild children of the bush. Now we come on a clearing in the bush, where two or three huts are all that remain to show the one-time thriving village of Brofu Edru. Villages of this name are frequent along the road. It means, literally, " the power of the white man "—indicating that the place was instituted when the white man had brought peace to the land in 1874. From this particular Brofu Edru we get our first view of the Adansi Mountains—merely a high bush-covered ridge rising above the surrounding trees, less than a mile away. Soon we commence the ascent. Almost direct the path climbs up—perhaps the straightest piece of road we have so far met with. Scarce a vestige remains of the beautiful zigzag way that was made by the Royal Engineers on the last campaign. As we rise, the air seems fresher, and much we want it, for never was the meaning so nearly brought home to us of the term "bathed in perspiration," as in our last efforts on the steamy flats. At length we reach the top—breathless and panting, longing for the view. But view there is none. All round us the same impenetrable bush, and where the foliage occasionally grants us a glimpse of the world beyond,

THE SCOUTS

we see a rolling expanse of tree-tops, looking sky-blue in the overhanging haze.

Now we descend down "Richmond Hill," past "Greenwich"— a stream where little fish like whitebait may be taken by using your mosquito curtain as a net. Suddenly a figure is before us, where a moment before was nothing but a curtain of bush—another scout stands glistening like a polished bronze statue in a sunlit spot. Again the cheery smile, bow, and handshake. He is one of the sentries from the neighbouring piquet. Already the horn is sounding, like a deep-toned steamer's whistle, to call the men together, and a few minutes later we are among them — good, cheery-looking bush-warriors, and well up to the work of keeping watch. Then we have a talk.

How they enjoy the palaver in which I tell them that "they are the eyes to the body of the snake which is crawling up the bush-path from the coast, and coiling for its spring! The eyes are hungry, but they will soon have meat; and the main body of white men, armed with the best of weapons, will help them win the day, and get their country back again, to enjoy in peace for ever." Then I show them my own little repeating rifle, and firing one shot after another, slowly at first, then faster and faster, till the four-

THE DOWNFALL OF PREMPEH

teen rounds roll off in a roar, I quite bring down the house. They crowd round jabbering and yelling, every man bent on shaking hands with the performer.

Later on we visit other piquets and their outposts. The sentries lie about within the bush close to any main paths, at such distance from the piquet as will allow of them being called in by the horn. Patrols of two men each go out along all paths for some eight or ten miles every day. At night the watch is kept by small parties of half a dozen men, who camp out on the paths a mile or two beyond the piquet. Like most natives, they will not work alone at night, but in small parties they do their night work admirably. Indeed, with such outposts in front of them, our expedition is pretty safe from any surprise by the enemy. Nor is their work by any means confined to passive watching, for far and wide, and well into the enemy's country, our scouts and spies have spread themselves — even in Kumassi itself. In this way not only are the actual moves of the Ashantis known to us, but also their every plan and preparation. At one piquet there stands a little group that interests us all. Two of the naked Adansi scouts have charge of a prisoner who is tied to one of them by a withe of monkey-creeper.

SCOUTING AT NIGHT

Page 88

THE SCOUTS

It is an Ashanti spy whom they have caught within the outpost line. An hour's interrogation gets little but contradictory statements from him, so he is remanded, under guard, for further inquiry. Other men are caught hiding in the bush, but evidently more fools than knaves, and they are sentenced to help in cutting the track and clearing the path. So, although at present we have not so far come to blows, life at the outpost is not altogether without its charm and interest.

IX

THE BEKWAI COLUMN

5th January 1896.

A NIGHT march is, as a rule, a slow and tedious business, unless there is some little excitement to enliven it. Last night we had the experience of a night march in which the spice of adventure relieved the tedium, although it did not, and indeed could not, do much towards making it a rapid one. The King of Bekwai, a tributary of Kumassi, had sent to the Governor messengers asking that he might come under the British flag, and that protection might at once be sent to him, as otherwise he would be taken by Prempeh and executed. A small flying column was therefore organised, and ordered to proceed at once from our outposts to the Bekwai capital, some twenty miles distant through the bush. The one road to it was held by an Ashanti piquet. The column was ordered to take a week's supplies, in order to

THE BEKWAI COLUMN

render it independent of its communications should it become cut off, in the defence of Bekwai, from the main body of the expedition. But this carrying of provisions, together with medical stores, ammunition, etc., involved the addition to its personnel of some 450 carriers, and as the whole force could only move in single file through the narrow jungle track, it may be imagined how great an incubus to its fighting efficiency was this long train of defenceless people. Even were the head of the column to succeed in driving the Ashanti piquet out of its position, the certainty was that the men composing it would scatter into the bush on either side of the track, and there lie ambushed until the non-combatant portion of the force came up before they opened fire. The effect on unarmed carriers —who by nature are at anyrate no braver, if half as brave, as most people—would have been excellent from the enemy's point of view, and would possibly have meant disaster to the little expedition. Moreover, the expedition was not a reconnaissance in force to drive in outposts, but rather a relief party, whose one object was to put itself as quickly as possible in touch with the place it was ordered to succour. It was therefore, determined to make a secret flank march

THE DOWNFALL OF PREMPEH

past the Ashanti outposts by night, and so gain a position where, on the one hand, we should be in touch with Bekwai, and, on the other, be in rear of the outpost, and so able to attack it with full advantage.

From Dompoassi, to reach Bekwai, the flying column would have to follow the Kumassi road as far as Esian Kwanta. At this point the Bekwai road branches off to the left; but it was at this same point that the Ashanti piquet was posted. About a mile away, to the left of Esian Kwanta, deep in the bush, is the village of Obum, connected with the Bekwai road by a path which joins it near Heman. This village, Obum, was not connected with the main Kumassi road until our scouts came and cut a path. And it was by this route, Obum and Heman, that the flank march was to be conducted. The flying column under my command was composed and formed as follows :—First, a section of the scouts ranging well to the front; then an advanced guard, followed by one company, headquarters, and drums of the Gold Coast Houssas, under command of Captain Mitchell. Then came the long string of carriers, among whom were distributed the Elmina company of my scouts for their better protection. Behind the carriers came a second

SPECIAL SERVICE CORPS ON THE MARCH TO BEKWAI

Page 92

THE BEKWAI COLUMN

company of Houssas, with a rearguard; and finally, in rear of all, another section of scouts, the whole comprising 700 men, and extending, when closed up, over a mile of path. No orders had been given to the force as to its march or destination till after dusk. It was then too late for would-be deserters to abscond; they would rather face the enemy with the crowd than venture alone on the ghost-haunted path that led homewards; and for the same reason, Ashanti spies, if there were any, having seen the camp apparently settle down for the night, would have gone back to report all quiet. We gave orders to parade at moonrise,—that was at a quarter to nine,—and shortly after that hour the column stood ready to proceed. In the bush-clearing, which is the site of the former town of Dompoassi, the rising moon, gleaming dully through the heavy night mist, gave sufficient light to show the long line of men standing motionless and dead silent—like a wall. The orders were given out and explained as to what was to be done by every man in the event of attack; ammunition was cast loose,—with no little pleasure on the part of the Houssas,—and presently the word was given to march—not that any word was heard, but the ghostly wall was seen to be slipping

THE DOWNFALL OF PREMPEH

quietly along to where it was lost in the dark tunnel of the bush.

And then began a night of trouble. Dark as pitch, one's only guide to the path was the white rag or package on the next man in front. With stick in hand, one groped one's way through the deep, dense gloom, hoping that as the moon rose things would improve—but they didn't. Buried in this bush, below the over-laced tree-tops, scarcely a ray could penetrate. Now a jerk down as one stepped off a hummock, now a stumble over a root, now caught in a prickly creeper, now ploughing through the holding swamp; and all around the deep silence of the forest, only broken by the rare crack of a trodden stick. One could scarcely believe that several hundred people were with one, moving—slowly, it was true, but still moving—ever forward. The carriers carried, in addition to their loads, their own packages of food and furniture—the furniture consisting of a mat, the food of plantains and dried fish. It was this dried fish that was my trouble. It was horrid; but one felt comforted to think that two atmospheres, namely, malaria and fish, could not have a place on that path together. Fallen trees were frequent, and tangled bush and streams combined to check and break the column. Each man

THE BEKWAI COLUMN

took his several seconds to negotiate the obstacle, and lost a few yards of distance in doing so, thus every minute saw the column growing longer. This could only be remedied by frequent halts and slow marching at the head. Occasionally the check would come from the head itself. Marching with the advance guard, there would be a sudden bump against the man in front of you, and, like a train of trucks, the whole party bumped to a standstill; then the whisper passed that the scouts had discovered the enemy. Suddenly a flicker and a flare of light in the bush well to our right. Enemy? No, it is the advanced scouts on our road, which twists and serpentines in a marvellous way, who think they have discovered an enemy's ambush. They creep around the particular thicket they suspect, then suddenly lighting brands, they hurl them into the hiding-place to light up the hoped-for target. This time they draw blank, and we move on again, grateful even for this little excitement. The march does not appear so tedious or so slow when one moves among the scouts. These fellows are on the *qui vive* all the time—now stopping to listen, now diving into the bush, with scarce a rustle, to search the flanks. Nor is their watchfulness too great for the occasion, for

THE DOWNFALL OF PREMPEH

twice we come upon the glowing logs of outpost fires that have hastily been quitted; but those are the only signs of men — whether friend or foe—being in the forest besides ourselves. At length the scouts creep forward, spreading out in an open clearing, and we reach the village of Obum. It is occupied by Bekwais, who, as they peer startled from their doors, tell us no Ashanti scouts are there. But we do not pause; clearings are more frequent, and consequently the light is better, and now we are on a well-worn path things seem better; but there is very little improvement in pace—the carriers are tired, and the column keeps ever trailing out.

It is long past two in the morning when our advanced guard reaches the village of Heman, and an hour later before the tail of the column comes in. Only nine miles in six hours, and everybody fagged! But we have gained our point; we have passed the outposts, and are in Bekwai country, within reach of the capital. We learn that the Ashantis have not yet advanced against it, and all is quiet. So after planting our outposts, we spread our beds in the verandahs which form the houses here, and roll off to sleep in no time. But it is not for long. Four hours' rest and a light breakfast set us up for further

THE BEKWAI COLUMN

work. One company of Houssas move off, with all the carriers, for Bekwai, some ten miles distant, while the remaining company, together with the scouts, prepare to turn on Esian Kwanta to clear the Ashantis out of it. The Houssas turn out with an eager alacrity that reminds one of our little warriors in other climes—the Ghoorkas. But once again, alas! their hopes are disappointed. The native scouts sent on ahead to reconnoitre Esian Kwanta come trotting back to tell us the enemy are not waiting for us to attack, but have bundled themselves out and away towards Kumassi. This renders the main road clear for those coming after us, and leaving a piquet of the scouts to occupy Esian Kwanta, we march away for Bekwai.

4th January.

One emerges from the shady forest on to a red, bare rising ground, on which are two long straggling streets of huts crossed by two others at right angles. Open and airy, but unimposing. This is Bekwai.

The Ashanti houses are similar in design to those of the Adansi country, in that a house usually consists of a collection of four small verandahs facing inwards, with walled backs.

THE DOWNFALL OF PREMPEH

They thus form a little court, with a small portico all round—not at all unlike the Pompeian houses, the more so as they are stuccoed with a smooth red-coloured cement. The houses differ in construction from those of the Adansis in being made of wattle and daub, and in having very high-pitched roofs. So long as the fine weather, with which we have luckily been blessed, continues, they form ideal houses for living in— shady, airy, and fairly clean.

Immediately on arrival of the flying column in Bekwai, I proceeded to the so-called palace, where I was received by the king in council, and after giving the king a letter assuring him of British protection, I received the evidently earnest thanks of the king for the prompt coming of the protecting force. The following morning (5th January) was devoted to the ceremony of hoisting the British flag, and small as the matter seemed to be at first, it developed into a very impressive function. African monarchs are very hard to hurry, but there was much business to be done, and business on an expedition such as this has to be done quickly. So that, after several messages requesting the king's wishes as to where and when the ceremony of hoisting the flag should take place, I had the staff set up in a

THE BEKWAI COLUMN

spot of my own choosing, paraded my force, and sent to tell the king that all was ready. This had the desired effect in the end, although the guard of honour of Houssas and of the B.P. Scouts had some time to wait before the din of drums and horns and the roaring of the crowd told that the royal procession was on the move. Presently it came in sight—a vast black crowd surging and yelling round the biers on which the king and chiefs were borne. Above and around them twirled the great state umbrellas. In front were bands of drummers with small drums, then dancing men who leaped and whirled along, fetish men in quaint head-dresses, drummers with kettledrums, trumpeters with their jaw-bedecked ivory horns, and then the great war-drums carried shoulder-high and hung with skulls, which were, however, for this occasion covered with a strip of cloth, signifying that it was a peace ceremony. There were the king's court criers with their tiny black and white caps, and running before and behind there rushed the crowd of slave boys carrying their masters' stools upon their heads. The roar and the drumming became intense as the procession came rushing up the road,—for it moved at a fast pace,—and the umbrellas whirling and leaping gave a great amount of life and

THE DOWNFALL OF PREMPEH

bustle to the scene. At last the throne and chairs were set, and the people marshalled by degrees into some kind of order. I then offered to the king the flag with all its advantages, which the king, with much spirit in his words, eagerly accepted; every phrase he used, besides being formally applauded by the chorus of court criers, was evidently fully approved of by the concourse.

The king then moved from his seat to the flagstaff. Though it was but a few paces, the move involved no small amount of ceremony. The umbrella had to be kept twirling over him while the bearer moved only on the ball of the foot. Men went before to clear every stick and straw from the royal path. The fetish man, in a handsome Red Indian kind of feather head-dress and a splendid silver belt, appeared to bless the scene. One man supported the king by holding his waist, and was himself similarly supported by two or three others in succession behind. Another mopped the king with a handkerchief, while boys armed with elephants' tails kept off stray flies from the royal presence. The king was dressed in a kind of patchwork toga with a green silk scarf, on his head a small tortoiseshell cap, and on his wrists, among the pendant fetish charms, he wore some splendid bracelets of rough

HOISTING THE FLAG AT BEKWAI

THE BEKWAI COLUMN

gold nuggets and human teeth. In all his barbaric splendour the king moved up to the flagstaff. The flag was at the masthead in a ball, and as he pulled the halyard that let it fall out in long gaudy folds, the band of the Houssas struck up "God save the Queen," and the troops presented arms. The king made a gesture as of going to sleep, with his head on his hand, and said that under that flag he should remain till he died. The officers of the Houssa force then came up and were introduced to the king. These were Captains Mitchell, Aplin, and Middlemist, Dr. Murray, etc.

Later in the day, the king and chiefs came in procession and called upon the British officers. This consisted in their filing past, bowing to each officer, and holding the hand out as if to bless him—the greater chiefs shaking hands. The king himself shook hands three or four times over with me, calling me his friend and deliverer, and then proceeded to favour the company with a few steps—a proceeding almost unprecedented in the annals of Bekwai, and intended as a very special compliment. This was the end of the ceremonial palaver; but later in the day there came a business palaver, the first of a series which lasted over the next two or three days,

THE DOWNFALL OF PREMPEH

whereat the king was asked to make some return for the privilege he now enjoyed of being a British subject, such as supplying men to act as carriers at a shilling a day, men to act as armed levies, assistance of villagers in cutting roads through the bush, and in supplying vegetable markets, etc. To each and every proposal he found some insuperable objection. A thousand carriers were required in two days' time; he could produce only two hundred in six days. Two thousand armed men were wanted to form a levy; he could only produce one thousand. This was accepted, and the thousand soldiers transferred to be carriers. He had not reckoned on that, so added they could not carry loads, did not know how, and could not be collected in less than ten days. Endless argument, promises of reward, only passed hours of fruitless talk.

"Was this the way he showed his gratitude for being saved from the Ashanti?"

"Yes; he was very sorry, but he could do no more."

"Very well, then, to-morrow the flag would be hauled down, and the troops would march away."

Thereupon, he thought that possibly six hundred carriers might be got in four days, and so

THE BEKWAI COLUMN

on, until at last all was promised as desired, and eventually the promises have been very fairly carried out. But it was a very wearisome business, this long preliminary haggling. The king too was generous in his way. A long string of slave boys brought us a pile of good things, such as yams, plantains, pawpaws, chickens, eggs, sheep, and even a bullock. And what a brute a man becomes after even a few weeks in the bush! We simply revelled in this fresh food. And yet, up to the present, we had had no cause to complain; modern "canning" science has shorn a campaign of much of its hardship; we are well supplied with Maconochie's rations, and as a great authority has said, "an army can go anywhere and do anything, so long as it possesses morale and Maconochie."

On the 5th January we were joined by a new white officer, Captain Williams, South Staffordshire Regiment, better known as "Litre-billee." He came to us practically for the purpose of replacing "The Sutler," who had at last fallen into the clutches of the fever fiend, and had to be sent into the newly established hospital at Qwisa. But "Litre-billee" was already ill when he reached us at Bekwai. And soon we heard that yet another officer, Captain Green of the Houssas, who had

THE DOWNFALL OF PREMPEH

been sent to command a wing of the levy then on a reconnaissance westward, had also been struck down, The fever, too, was not of a kind that had a set-to with you and then retired, but after giving a shattering blow, he hung around and kicked at you at intervals; so that these officers, after their first seizure, were never up to the mark again, although between the attacks they went to work as energetically as ever.

6th January.

This day was enlivened by an incident which, small as it was in itself, had a large effect on our dealings with the King of Bekwai. My report to the Assistant Adjutant-General thus briefly describes it all:—

"I received this morning your orders to stop communications between the King of Bekwai and messengers from the people at the coast or at Kumassi.

"I accordingly sent out piquets on the roads; and hearing that two native clerks had just arrived from the south, simultaneously with some envoys from Kumassi, and that all were about to confer with King Bekwai, I marched half a company of Houssas to the king's house, surrounded it, called him out, and ordered him to hand to me the

THE BEKWAI COLUMN

strangers. This he did, and I have them under guard in different houses. Neither the Cape Coast men nor the Ashantis have had any interview with the king. Two of the king's men tried to escape during the arrest, but were captured by the Houssas at the back of the 'palace.'"

This somewhat high-handed procedure evidently startled the king, and showed him that we did not blindly believe in him. The result was that from that hour he exerted himself, and carried out fully one-half of his promises.

While at Bekwai, we have been joined by Prince Christian Victor and Major Piggott, who have come up to see the place, and who evidently mean to make themselves welcome to headquarters when they return with the numbers of fowls and eggs they are purchasing from the natives.

X

Forward Movements

ON 8th January we interviewed a party of envoys sent from Kumassi to ask us to delay, if not to abandon, our advance upon that place. Then, after a run back down to the road to report progress at headquarters (which were now at Qwisa), I pressed on with the levy in continuation of our work of road-making. One good I got out of my hurried trip to headquarters was, that I obtained the valuable services of Major Gordon, 15th Hussars, for the levy, in lieu of Captain Graham and the others who were still sick; but a cloud hung over that day, as I heard of the death, at Prahsu, of poor Victor Ferguson, Royal Horse Guards. "Beloved by all" stands true for him. And Prince Henry too was just struck down, and lying sick in camp.

15th January.

We have pushed on from day to day, bush-

FORWARD MOVEMENTS

cutting, camp-building, bridging, and corduroying in the never-changing, never-ending forest. On the further bank of the Ordah River we clear a large amount of bush, to form a field of fire for a rough bridgehead, which we hastily construct of brushwood—for 'tis here we might expect to be opposed, as happened in 1874. Indeed, so hopeful are the troops at this point that the noise of our axes as we were felling trees brought up the Special Service Corps at the double, since it sounded like the dropping fire of rifles. It was here, too, that "The Sutler" reappeared, pale from his bed of sickness, but resolved to be with us for the advance on Kumassi. And how our "red-caps" cheered to see him with them once again!

At Ordasu once more we meet an embassy from Prempeh. To Captain Donald Stewart, our Political Officer, they offer his submission—complete and unconditional. Alas! this looks like a peaceful end of all our work. Yet at the moment there have been the makings of a row. A panic among the attendants of the envoys induced a rush into the bush, and as they blundered through our active outposts, the latter, naturally thinking something wrong, started in chase, and chairs and stools, state swords and oof-bags were

THE DOWNFALL OF PREMPEH

dropped in wild confusion. But confidence was soon restored, losses made good, and the summary punishment of one or two detected looting put all on friendly terms again.

Yet, in spite of all assurances, we cannot trust to what Ashantis say. We know their warriors are not far away, and every care must still be taken as we near Kumassi.

The following is the formation ordered for our final advance into the place :—

The levy, being now 860 strong, is able to find two flanking parties on by-roads to the town, in addition to its main party on the central road.

Baden-Powell's Command.

Advanced Guard. { ☐ } Two Companies Gold Coast Houssas and Maxim.

Distance, quarter mile, communication kept up by men dropped by the Gold Coast Houssas.

FORWARD MOVEMENTS

	Special Service Corps.
† † †	Two guns. Maxim.
	Headquarters Staff.
	Half Bearer Company.
	Six Companies 2nd West Yorkshire Regiment
† † † †	Two guns. Two rockets.
	Half Bearer Company.
	Ammunition Column.
	Baggage Column.
	Supply Column.
	Field Hospital.
	Two Companies 2nd West Yorkshire Regiment.
	Lagos Houssas, with Maxim.

Nearly nine miles long.

Rear Guard. { Two Companies 2nd West Yorkshire Regiment. / Lagos Houssas, with Maxim. }

} One Company 2nd West India Regiment distributed by half sections through this portion of the column.

XI

IN KUMASSI

KUMASSI, *January* 17.

KUMASSI at last! And what a disappointment! For a long and toilsome march to end in a scene of such meanness and squalor; for a well-equipped, expensive expedition to have attained its goal with so very little return to show for it—all contribute to depress everybody with a feeling of bitter disappointment rather than with the high elation that had been hoped for. Especially hard has it been on the men in the ranks. For weeks past they have been borne up by the one hope—they have struggled on—more than manfully—against all the evils of the climate and the country. Through the endless, sickly forest they have dragged on mile after mile, literally fighting down leg-weariness and fever; every man meaning to be "in it" when the fight came off; and after that—well, they didn't care whether they lived or

BIRD'S-EYE VIEW OF KUMASSI

1. Headquarters. 2. Special Service Corps. 3. Field hospital. 4. Transport Corps. 5. Sacred tree and fetish buildings, Bantama. 6. Baden-Powell's levies, Bantama. 7. West Indian Regiment. 8. Prumeh's palace. 9. Sacred fetish grove. 10. Bush cleared round palace enclosure. 11. Queen Mother's house. 12. West Yorkshire Regiment. 13. Palaver ground. 14. Execution place. 15. Royal Engineers. 16. Royal Artillery. 17. Grove where bodies of victims of sacrifice were thrown. 18. Gold Coast Hausas. 19. Sherri River.

Page 110

IN KUMASSI

died—better perhaps to get bowled over by the fever then, as it would mean riding in a hammock back to the coast. But as things now stand, even without the fight, the expense will be the same in valuable lives and good constitutions lost.

All yesterday my force was working its way by three different paths towards the capital. Here and there we captured armed Ashantis watching in the bush, but no kind of resistance was offered to the advance, One curious incident occurred to waken up those spirits of the main body who had begun to despair of getting a fight. Major Gordon was commanding the right flank party of the advanced force. A crumpled scrap of paper arrived by a native runner from this part of the command, bearing the ominous words—

"Major Gordon
"Killed 14th inst."

This, of course, caused much discussion and rumour in the camp, till someone discovered a faint pencil note of receipt initialed by Major Gordon himself, and it then was remembered that a piece of fresh meat had been sent off to him a day or two previously, with this selfsame label attached to it.

A few miles in rear of my crew came the main

THE DOWNFALL OF PREMPEH

body, headed by Houssas and the Special Service Corps, and, with its long string of supply, ammunition, and hospital columns, it covered something like nine miles of road.

The duty of the advanced force was to scout and to cut the road for the main body, but there was now no time for building huts, as had been the practice up till now; accordingly the troops had to make their own bush-shelters or pitch their *tentes d'abri.*

Most unfortunately a tornado paid us a visit last night. A violent thunderstorm and torrents of rain lasting several hours played havoc with the slight, improvised shelters, and turned everybody out in good time for an early start, but as wet and bedraggled as it was possible for men to be. Still, as usual, the wetter and more miserable his surroundings, the more cheery is Tommy Atkins, and to-day was to be the last of the march. Reports were flying around that the enemy meant to oppose us at the gates of Kumassi, to make one stand there, and if beaten, to blow up the city, and disperse into the bush. "Gates," "city," "king's palace"; all sounded well, but what did we find?

Through dense, high elephant grass, along a little beaten foot-path—which was strewn with

IN KUMASSI

fetish dolls—we got near to the place. As our scouts warily approached, the drums could be heard rumbling and booming far and near. Presently we passed a cluster of the usual mud huts, then another; several other clusters were in sight, with patches of high jungle grass between. Then a bare open patch of ground 200 yards across, with huts about, and more thatched roofs in the hollow beyond.

This was Kumassi.

With Graham and myself and our scouts came Captain Donald Stewart, the Political Officer, and Major Piggott, with the Union Jack on a silver-mounted hog-spear. Then came the native levies, followed by a company of Houssas with their drums and fifes, under Captain Mitchell. Within a few minutes of our arrival there appeared from the right of the town Major Gordon's flank detachment, and shortly after from the left a similar party of the levy, who had cut their way through the bush where no road lay. So that, had the enemy resisted the entrance of the centre main column, he would have found himself immediately attacked on both flanks simultaneously, and the fight, had there been one, could not have lasted long. The advanced force now formed itself upon the so-called parade-ground, and sent

THE DOWNFALL OF PREMPEH

piquets on beyond the town to guard approaches, while the main body was moving up from out the bush.

The drumming in the town was getting louder, and the roar of voices filled the air; but, alas! it was peace drumming. The great coloured umbrellas were soon seen dancing and bobbing above the heads of the surging crowds of natives. Stool-bearers ran before, then came the whirling dancers with their yellow skirts flying round them. Great drums, like beer-barrels, decked with human skulls, were booming out their notes, and bands of elephant-tusk horns were adding to the din. The king and all his chiefs were coming out to see the troops arrive. Presently they arranged themselves in a dense long line. The umbrellas formed a row of booths, beneath which the chiefs sat on their brass-nailed chairs, with all their courtiers round them. This was nine o'clock, and there they sat till five.

Often had they sat like this before upon that same parade-ground; but never had their sitting been without the sight of blood. The object of this open space was not for parading troops, but for use as the theatre of human sacrifice. Orders had been given before our arrival to clean away all signs of this custom, nor were the people

King Prempeh watching the arrival of troops

IN KUMASSI

to speak of it to the white men; but with very little cross-examination all the facts came out. Indeed, while standing about the parade-ground, "The Sutler" peered into the coppice close by, where the trees supported a flock of healthy-looking vultures, and there at once he found skulls and bones of human dead.

And there sits Prempeh, looking very bored, as three scarlet-clad dwarfs dance before him, amid the dense crowd of sword-bearers, court criers, fly-catchers, and other officials. He looks a regal figure as he sits upon a lofty throne with a huge velvet umbrella standing over him, upon his head a black and gold tiara, and on his neck and arms large golden beads and nuggets. Presently a little party of our force comes hurriedly across the ground, three white soldiers with four natives carrying a reel and winding off the field telegraph; and thus within a few minutes practically of the arrival of the advanced force in Kumassi, the fact would have been known at home had not the previous day's tornado destroyed the line in sundry places. But this feat has not been performed without cost. Of the telegraph section, Captain Curtis is in hospital with fever, as are also many of his men; and it is a fact worthy of record how, in spite of this and of the heavy

THE DOWNFALL OF PREMPEH

work connected with the laying and the working of the line, its completion has been carried out with such rapidity and efficiency.

The billeting officers sent forward under Colonel Ward, the Assistant Adjutant - General for B duties, have been busy in allotting different portions of the town to the various units of the force as quarters, so that no time need be lost in housing them on their arrival.

And presently they come. The advanced guard of the Houssas lead the way.

Then come the Special Service Corps. Wet, and white of face, but going strong and well, they march up in their little companies to their places on parade, amid the admiring cheers of those of us who were already there to greet them. Close behind the 7-pounder guns came up, carried on bamboo poles.

And then Sir Francis Scott and staff, all looking hale and well. In rear of these there marches in the West Yorkshire Regiment, all ranks of most soldierly and most workmanlike appearance. A thousand pities that there is so little for them to do!

No time is lost. The billeting officers show the way, and soon the units are filing off to their various quarters about the town, the advanced

IN KUMASSI

force continuing its move to a mile beyond the town—to Bantama.

Later in the afternoon, Sir Francis Scott, with all his staff, seated in a semicircle on the parade-ground, received a visit from King Prempeh and his chiefs. There had been some conjectures as to what Prempeh might do when asked to come down from his throne to meet the commander of the troops, but he came down without a word; indeed, it looks as though the Ashantis had agreed to give in to their visitors on every point that might be raised — until their backs are turned!

The usual long string of chiefs, each with his little court, came thronging by, saluting with outstretched hand the officers; and finally King Prempeh came himself, supported and even jostled by his swarming courtiers, his flabby yellow face glistening with oil, and his somewhat stupid expression rendered more idiotic by his sucking a large nut like a fat cigar.

Sir Francis told him in plain terms that he would have to make his submission in accordance with native forms and customs to the Governor, who would shortly arrive in Kumassi. Beyond that he did not enter on political questions, but merely gave a few necessary orders regarding

THE DOWNFALL OF PREMPEH

the provision of markets and the maintenance of order, etc., and the interview came to an end.

The queen-mother followed, and looked a good-natured, smiling little woman; but beneath that smile she is said, like others of her sex, to hide a store of villainy.

XII

Preparing the "Coup"

20th January.

A VERY lively day to-day was preceded by almost as lively a night. It was known that some of the leading chiefs now in Kumassi, and even Prempeh himself, might endeavour to slip away during the night; therefore every road and bush-path leading out of the place was quietly piqueted by our levy. During the day piquets had been posted on all the main paths, more for protecting villagers bringing in supplies to the market than for any defensive purposes. But after dark these piquets were strengthened, and extra ones were added to prevent egress as well as ingress by natives.

It was soon evident, from the prisoners whom the outposts secured, that the palace people were anxiously reconnoitring the various roads, only to find them all barred. John Ansah was seen by

THE DOWNFALL OF PREMPEH

several of the piquets, and was finally captured by one posted on a by-path leading from the palace to the bush.

In the evening a council had been hastily summoned at the palace, and it sat nearly all the night.

After going round all the piquets, we put out our torches, and went as what is termed a "hanging patrol"—a party of men who "hang about" for a few minutes here and for an hour there, as the commander may deem desirable.

Our hanging about was chiefly near the palace. Twice we visited the sacred fetish grove, in front of it, where some newly-turned earth made one suspicious of hidden treasure that they might think necessary to dig up and remove to safer quarters.

Then we went and squatted in the shadow of some huts, and had hardly settled ourselves when a gleam of light came from the palace doorway, and a procession with torches issued forth? Was it Prempeh making off? The time was now three o'clock, and there was a thick, wet mist. The string of white-robed figures, looking most picturesque in the strong light of the torches, drew silently near, and then we saw, from the big hand-screen carried by the attend-

Capture of one of Prempeh's Scouts by the Author

PREPARING THE "COUP"

ants, that the queen-mother was the leading notability in the group. Silently they passed up a by-street within twenty yards of us, and very softly we followed them until we had marked them down into the queen's residence. Then back to our ambush. In a few minutes more a councillor on his way home, attended by a slave boy carrying his stool, walked into our midst. He was too startled to speak before he had been told that silence would save his life. Soon a fast-footed pair of men were heard pattering up. Just as they came close upon us, they suspected something. One of them stood within arm's length of me, peering into the darkness in the opposite direction. I stood up, and he did not move. I reached out and got hold of him, and luckily gripped the gun he was carrying. Others of the patrol were on to him in a moment, but he fought like a maniac, wriggling and twisting till he got one hand free and dived it into the back of his skirt; but he was pinned in good time, and a handsome knife in a leopard-skin scabbard was added to our spoil.

His companion had meantime made a dash for liberty, but was tripped up and caught by a couple of quick Adansis. He proved to be a servant carrying his master's spare clothes and bedding.

THE DOWNFALL OF PREMPEH

Hardly had these been stowed in the shade, ere an old man was heard coming slowly, slippperty-slop in his sandals, evidently loafing home after the council. We sat silent, and he passed between our ranks without ever dreaming that he was within arm's length of a dozen enemies. One or two more councillors fell into our hands, and then réveillé began to sound in one camp after another round the town; strings of water-carriers began to pass our lurking-place; the mist grew lighter overhead, and our night-watch was over. Prisoners were separately examined and released—the armed man minus his gun, sword, and knife; and soon we were back in camp, breakfasting with the keenest of appetites, and cheered by the knowledge that we had got Prempeh and the queen-mother "marked down" all safe for the morning's doings.

XIII

THE DOWNFALL

20th January.

NOR were these long in beginning. Six o'clock had been named as the hour for Prempeh and all his chiefs to be on the palaver-ground. This was done, well knowing that he might then be expected about seven, and it was desirable to make an early start with the ceremony, in order not to keep the white troops exposed to the sun in the middle of the day. Soon after seven o'clock the troops began to form up on the parade-ground, but still no sign of any of the Ashantis coming; nor even was there any of the usual preliminary drumming that invariably goes on to summon all the retainers who usually form the procession.

Nearly two hours' grace had been given him; it looked as though Prempeh did not mean coming. The order was accordingly given for the Special Service Corps, assisted by the native levy, to

THE DOWNFALL OF PREMPEH

surround the palace and the queen-mother's house, and to bring Prempeh and the queen to the Governor. Captain D. Stewart went in to "draw" them.

The native levy, in view of such course becoming necessary, had during the previous day cut away the bush adjoining the palace enclosure, and thus the cordon was enabled rapidly to take up its position to close every outlet.

In a very few minutes the king was carried forth in his state cradle with a small following, and, escorted by the troops, he proceeded hurriedly to the palaver-ground. The queen-mother, similarly escorted, followed shortly after, as well as all the chiefs. They were then marshalled in a line, with a limited number of attendants each, in front of the Governor, Mr. Maxwell, C.M.G., who was seated on a dais, together with Colonel Sir Francis Scott, K.C.B., and Colonel Kempster, D.S.O.

A square of British troops was formed all round, backed by Houssas and the native levy.

Then the doom of the nation was pronounced in a set-scene, and amid dramatic incidents such as could not fail to impress both natives and Europeans alike.

Through the medium of interpreters — Mr.

PALAVER AND SUBMISSION OF KING PREMPEH

THE DOWNFALL

Vroom, Secretary for Native Affairs, acting for the Governor; Albert Ansah, for the king—the conditions of the treaty to be imposed upon the Ashantis were demanded of them.

The first of these was that Prempeh should render submission to the Governor, in accordance with the native form and custom signifying abject surrender. This is a ceremony which has only once before been carried out between the Ashantis and a British Governor, namely, Governor Rowe. On that occasion the king deputed officers of his court to perform the actual ceremony; but in this case it was insisted that the king must himself personally carry it out.

Accordingly, with bad enough grace, he walked from his chair, accompanied by the queen-mother, and, bowing before Mr. Maxwell, he embraced his knees. It was a little thing, but it was a blow to the Ashanti pride and prestige such as they had never suffered before.

Then came the demand for payment of the indemnity for the war. Due notice had been previously given, and the Ashantis had promised to pay it; but unless the amount, or a fair proportion of it, could now be produced, the king and his chiefs must be taken as guarantee for its payment.

THE DOWNFALL OF PREMPEH

The king could produce about a twentieth part of what had been promised. Accordingly, he was informed that he, together with his mother and chiefs, would now be held as prisoners, and deported to the Gold Coast.

The sentence moved the Ashantis very visibly. Usually it is etiquette with them to receive all news, of whatever description, in the gravest and most unmoved indifference; but here was Prempeh bowing himself to the earth for mercy, as doubtless many and many a victim to his lust for blood had bowed in vain to him, and around him were his ministers on their feet, clamouring for delay and reconsideration of the case. The only "man" among them was the queen.

In vain. Each chief found two stalwart British non-commissioned officers at his elbow, Prempeh being under charge of Inspector Donovan. Their arrest was complete.

But there was still an incident coming to complete the scene. The two Ansahs, although they held a large hand in causing the trouble between the British and Ashantis, appear in their own country to have little or no influence with the people, and, indeed, were looked on with jealousy and suspicion. These were surveying the scene —their handiwork—with a somewhat curious

Submission of King Prempeh, January 20th, 1896

Page 126

THE DOWNFALL

look, half amused, half nonplussed, when the Governor added to his remarks the suggestion that the present might be a suitable occasion for the arrest of these two gentlemen on a charge of forgery; and before they had fully realised between them that the charge was actually being preferred against them, they found that Mr. Donovan had adroitly handcuffed them wrist to wrist, and the scene was complete.

During the performance of this act another had been quietly preparing behind the scenes. Parties of the native levy had been withdrawn from the parade-ground, and were added to the cordon already drawn round the palace. All was silent there, and all the many doors were locked. But a path from the jungle leading to the back door, also locked, brought one within sound of the buzz of many men talking within, and of the soughing of bellows of smelting fires. At the close of the palaver on the parade-ground, two companies of the West Yorkshire Regiment, under Captain Walker, were detailed to take possession of the palace, clear it of all people inside, and to collect and make an inventory of all property found inside.

One company was accordingly sent to stiffen the cordon of native levies, and with the other

THE DOWNFALL OF PREMPEH

company I proceeded to effect an entrance by a back way, which I had previously reconnoitred.

There had been reports of the palace being undermined, and it was natural to expect that if this was so, the main entrance would be the spot selected for the mine, and that at any rate the place where the inmates were collected would be safe. Accordingly, making its way through the deserted garden, this company proceeded to the back entrance, and burst open the door. This opened into a large courtyard. Not a soul to be seen! Everything silent. Two painted doors in a side wall were kicked in by soldiers, and immediately after Tommy Atkins' persuasive voice was sounding, "Come out of that, you blatherskiting idiot; d'ye think I want to eat you?" and so on, as a frightened flock of natives were dragged out into the daylight. They were placed in the courtyard under sentries, while the remainder of the company proceeded to search every corner of every court and alley of the palace—and these were many—for further occupants. A hundred or two of these were taken, and then the work of collecting valuables and property was proceeded with.

There could be no more interesting, no more tempting work than this. To poke about in a

THE DOWNFALL

barbarian king's palace, whose wealth has been reported very great, was enough to make it so. Perhaps one of the most striking features about it was that the work of collecting the treasures was entrusted to a company of British soldiers, and that it was done most honestly and well, without a single case of looting. Here was a man with an armful of gold-hilted swords, there one with a box full of gold trinkets and rings, another with a spirit-case full of bottles of brandy, yet in no instance was there any attempt at looting.

It need not be supposed that all the property found in the palace was of great value. There were piles of the tawdriest and commonest stuff mixed indiscriminately with quaint, old, and valuable articles, a few good brass dishes, large metal ewers, Ashanti stools, old arms, etc. But a large amount of valuables known to belong to the king had disappeared, probably weeks previously—such as his celebrated dinner service of Dutch silver, his golden hat, his golden chair of state, and, above all, the royal stool, the emblem *par excellence* of the King of Ashanti.

These were all probably hidden, together with his wives, in various hamlets in the remote bush. The "loot" which we collected was sold by

THE DOWNFALL OF PREMPEH

public auction, excepting golden valuables, which were all sent home to the Secretary of State.

The term "palace" has merely been used to denote the residence of the king. In reality there is very little that is palatial about it. It consists of a collection of the usual wattle-and-daub huts, with high walls and enormous high-pitched thatched roofs; endless courts, big and little, succeed each other, with narrow entries between, and with little or no attempt at architectural design or ornamentation.

The foundations of the old palace, built on more substantial principles, and destroyed in the last campaign, are still to be seen in the centre of the present place in a disused court.

Finding so little of real value in the palace, it was hoped that some treasure might be discovered in the sacred fetish-houses at Bantama, the burial-place of the kings of Ashanti, about a mile out of Bantama. This place had also been piqueted, but all its priests had disappeared previously, and when we broke in, only one harmless old man was found residing there. No valuables—in fact, little of any kind was found in the common huts that form the sacred place. In the big fetish building, with its enormous thatched roof, when burst open, we only found

THE DOWNFALL

a few brass coffers—all empty! The door, which was newly sealed with mortar, showed no signs of having been quite freshly closed up, and it may therefore be inferred that the treasure had been removed some weeks previously.

Then, in accordance with orders, we set the whole of the fetish village in flames, and a splendid blaze it made. The great fetish-tree, in whose shade hundreds of victims have been sacrificed, was blown up with gun-cotton, as also were the great fetish-trees on the Kumassi parade-ground. Among the roots of these there lie the skulls and bones of hundreds, and possibly of thousands, of victims to the *régime* which to-day has so dramatically been brought to a close.

XIV

AFTER EVENTS

KUMASSI, 22*nd January*.

IT has given us some amusement here to read the statements of Mr. Hogan and others who, according to the last received budget of papers, have been enlightening the British public on the subject of Ashanti. They have, however, condemned themselves out of their own mouth, their prophecies have been altogether stultified by the outcome of events, and their general statements are equally wide of facts. Prempeh and his chiefs did not escape into the interior, partly because steps were taken to prevent them doing so, and chiefly because up to the last they had not been sure of the line that they would adopt. That the Ashantis would not fight could not have been foreseen, but could only have been guessed at, as subsequent events have shown.

It is now known that had it not been for the

AFTER EVENTS

presence of the two white battalions in the expeditionary force, the Ashantis would have attacked, and might very possibly have stopped any column sent up. Eight thousand men had been collected in Kumassi only ten days before our arrival there, and are to-day not altogether disbanded. They were, as our scouts reported, waiting about in neighbouring villages ready for the call of their chiefs, who were in Kumassi. But the *coup* of Mr. Maxwell in arresting in full palaver the king, queen-mother, and all the leading chiefs has utterly demoralised them, and the nation is now like a flock of sheep without a leader. Had the people even guessed beforehand what the result of the *coup* was to have been, there is not the smallest doubt that they would have fought to prevent it.

When we arrived here on the 17th inst., Kumassi was full of its ordinary inhabitants. On the 19th, there was suspicion in the air. Numbers were trying to make their way out of the town; all the fetish priests at Bantama fled; there is little doubt, had the roads and the palace not been carefully guarded all that night, that Prempeh and other important personages would have been missing in the morning. By the evening of the 20th, the day of the arrest, there

THE DOWNFALL OF PREMPEH

was not a soul left in Kumassi. With his characteristic promptness the Governor intimated that the force could now move down again, taking with it its string of prisoners, and on the 21st orders were issued for the move next day. A prison had been improvised by isolating a suitable collection of huts near the headquarters camp. All surrounding houses were levelled to the ground, and a guard was mounted to make it secure on all sides. Precautions had also to be taken, not only against escape or rescue, but against the suicide or assassination of the king; the disgrace, and more especially fetish and superstition, made it desirable to the king and to his people that he should not be removed alive from Kumassi.

Yesterday evening (the 21st) more reports came in of armed men being in neighbouring villages, and there were whisperings of possible reconnaissances during the night. Bantama, about a mile and a half from Kumassi, was the headquarters of the levy, and it was there, at two in the morning of to-day, I paraded a reconnoitring force—four companies of the scouts under Major Gordon, two companies of Houssas under Captain Mitchell, a Maxim gun in charge of Armourer-Sergeant Williams. Then we

AFTER EVENTS

started : a long, silent string of men gliding past the outposts of the troops in camp, down through the deserted lanes of Kumassi, and out into the bush beyond. Suddenly our path becomes muddy, and then watery—we try to keep dryshod, but in vain ; ere long we are ankle-deep, then knee-deep, and deeper, and so we wade on and on through the cold and evil-smelling water swamps that lie below Kumassi.

Once past it, our way lies through the densest bush by a narrow, winding foot-track, whose line we guess at by feeling with a stick. Streams, fallen trees, and high-growing roots obstruct our way at every step, and our progress naturally is extremely slow, and, cold and miserable about the legs, we creep along. Hour after hour, mile after mile, in deepest silence ; frequent halts while scouts examine points ahead, or to allow some closing up in rear. At last the dawn begins to show itself in the thick and dripping mist around us. The men all have their orders what to do on arrival at the village. The scouts will gain both flanks through the bush, followed by a section to either hand of Houssas ; the Maxim takes the centre with the remainder of the Houssas, while the rest of the levy face about and guard the rear. The ammunition is ready,

THE DOWNFALL OF PREMPEH

and we really hope that now at least a brush will be our reward.

Presently the scouts bring in a capture, a wild-looking native talking in a strange up-country tongue. He is a slave, who has just made his escape from a village near our path, and which at this moment is full of armed Ashantis; but it is not the place we came to take. Here we know that 400 men are mustered, and so we press on faster in the gradually lightening gloom. Now we are near, the scouts check to reconnoitre, and the column closes up on tiptoe. Forward! A cry from the scouts. Too late! They've gone; got wind of our coming, and the place is empty. Nothing for it but to munch our biscuit and chocolate, and after a few minutes' rest to march our weary way back—back through the bush, back through the long, wet, fœtid swamp, and so to the camp.

Here we find the tail of the column just moving out upon its downward march, and we prepare to form the rearguard. But other orders wait us. Another village has just been reported to be full of men and treasure, so, after an hour's rest and breakfast, once more the scouts turn out, and, backed by a fresh company of Houssas, proceed to visit the newly-designated point. Once more

AFTER EVENTS

we ford the filthy swamp, which, with its repeated stirrings by many feet, has now "a fine old crusted" reek. Luckily we have not far to go—two miles will bring us there. A running scout was sent before to spy the place, and presently he meets us with the news we half expected—the enemy have gone, leaving five men there and heaps of boxes. So we press on silently. Our scouts capture one of theirs without a sound. Then we rush the village, and catch three men who have hidden away their arms. Among the huts lie strewn a host of boxes broken and empty. Within the little courtyards are piles of articles in jumbled-up confusion. The place itself was Prempeh's country house, and his furniture was chiefly feather-beds, plates, dishes, and despatch-boxes. Delft of the commonest make strews the place, and is evidently looked upon as valuable by our men, who, after asking leave, proceed to pile themselves up with the largest dishes they can find. The place looks like a jumble auction sale. Old chairs and curtains, common decanters, a bust of her Majesty, common cotton cloths, gin bottles in profusion. At first it looked as though a hurried attempt at packing up had been made by the inmates, but one of our prisoners told another

THE DOWNFALL OF PREMPEH

tale. Valuables and jewellery had been securely packed in all the boxes here and placed in charge of a Sefwi slave, the king's head drummer. The day before our arrival, this man had come, with others of his tribe, and had systematically looted the whole of the valuables, and was by this time miles away, hidden in the bush.

Once more we turned back to the camp, a disappointed crew. And on arrival there we found the Union Jack was flying half-mast high. Good Prince Henry! a martyr, if ever there was martyr, to his sense of duty. And then we started on our coastward march, not as we had pictured it, light-hearted and rejoicing, but tired and disappointed, and very sick at heart at this last crowning blow.

XV

THE COASTWARD MARCH

PRAHSU, 26*th January.*

THE retreat is generally more fatal than the advance. In its retirement from Kumassi the expeditionary force has still had the same two foes to contend against that it had in the advance up to that place. On the one hand, it had to be prepared against the Ashantis, on the other hand, against fever.

The danger from Ashantis on the return journey lay in any attempt that might be made to effect the rescue of their king or of one or more of their chiefs from the custody of the English, or, failing a rescue, in the endeavour which it was more than probable they would make to assassinate Prempeh. It would be a great blow to the prestige of the Ashanti nation, and destructive of the one national superstition, if the king were to be taken even across the

THE DOWNFALL OF PREMPEH

Sberri river, which surrounds Kumassi, and then on, altogether out of the country. So that as long as he was still in Kumassi, or in Ashanti territory, there was every chance that an attempt would be made, if rescue were impossible, even by single individuals to take the king's life. Nor would there be an end to this danger when he had passed out of Ashanti territory, for then he would travel through first the Bekwai and later the Adansi countries, where people were quite as ready to shoot him, although from another cause, namely, from a desire to pay off old scores and wipe out the blood of relations who had been the victims of sacrifice at some of the king's "customs." The narrow path that constitutes the "Great North Road," and the dense bush hedging either side of it, affords a perfect cover for such ambuscade, whether of an individual or of even a large body; consequently special precautions had to be taken to make all secure for the safe passage of the prisoner. He was escorted by white troops on the path, while all the by-paths for miles round were occupied by piquets of the levy, and the bush itself was thoroughly searched by them, previous to and during the passage of the convoy of prisoners. The levy also visited outlying villages, where

THE COASTWARD MARCH

gatherings of armed men were reported, and drove them off in all directions. There was plenty of evidence that the precautions taken were no more than were necessary, and the additional toil was compensated by the entire success of this our last task of the campaign.

The other enemy—the fever—was not defeated with such success. Since turning its back on Kumassi for the coastward march, the force has come to feel the clutch of sickness. The weather is no worse than it was for the march up-country. It is, in fact, even more healthy just now, and the men themselves, after their long march, should now be in far better, harder condition than when fresh landed, soft from shipboard life. It is, therefore, not so much from physical causes that the men are becoming a prey to sickness; it is rather due to mental depression. It is the result of the feeling of absolute disappointment which now pervades the force. They have worked hard, marching through the poisonous tangle of rank forest and swamp, bearing up under the enervating heat, and fighting against sickness, simply with the pluck and determination that are characteristic of the Briton bent on achieving the task he has set before himself. To see the Special Service Corps, at the end of a long day's

THE DOWNFALL OF PREMPEH

march, suddenly prick up their ears, as it were, and press on at the double because they thought they heard firing in front, was a sight that may well be recorded. Their one idea has been to get at the enemy to give him a real good drubbing; and whatever may be said of the morality of such an aspiration, none the less it spurs Tommy Atkins to great deeds, that so he may win the medal. Now all their hopes and all their aspirations are dashed to the ground. Wearied and dispirited, they are now dragging their way back along the hateful, depressing road, and between them and the coast there lie many miles of malarial bush, through which but few can pass untouched by the poison in the air. But they plod along pluckily through the fœtid forest. As I passed one loaded hammock among the many on the line of march to-day, a haggard, bearded face within looked out with burning eyes, and the sick man asked, "Do you think, sir, they will give us a medal for this?" At my "No doubt they will," he sank back in some relief to dream it over. The men have suffered and endured even more than if they had had fighting, for the consequent excitement would have carried them through much that affects them now.

THE COASTWARD MARCH

Cape Coast Castle, 8*th February* 1896.

The march up to Kumassi was a weary, toilsome business, even in spite of the excitement and hope which buoyed the men up. What, then, can one say of the march down, when the same long depressing road had to be re-traversed by men whose spirits were now lowered by the deep disappointment they had suffered, and whose systems were gradually giving in to the attacks of the ever-present fever fiend? In truth, that march down was in its way as fine an exhibition of British stamina and pluck as any that has been seen of late years. For the casual reader in England this is difficult to realise, but to one who has himself wearily tramped that interminable path, heartsick and footsore, the sight of those dogged British "Tommies," heavily accoutred as they were, still defying fever in the sweltering heat, and ever pressing on, was one which opened one's eyes and one's heart as well.

There was no malingering *there*; each man went on until he dropped. It showed more than any fight could have done, more than any investment in a fort, or surprise in camp, what stern and sterling stuff our men are made of, notwith-

THE DOWNFALL OF PREMPEH

standing all that cavillers will say against our modern army system and its soldiers.

To one fine young fellow—who, though evidently gripped by fever, still was doggedly marching on—I suggested that his kit was very heavy, whereat he replied, with the tight drawn smile and quavering voice one knows too well out here, "It ain't the kit, sir! it's only these extra rounds that I feel the weight of." "These extra rounds" being those intended for the fight which never came. The never-ending sameness of the forest was in itself sufficient to depress the most light and cheerful mind, and thus it was a great relief at length to get to Mansu, where the bush begins to open out, and where there is more of the light and air of heaven. But the change is not altogether for the better. The forest, it is true, is gone, but the road is open to the sun, while the undergrowth on either hand is denser now than ever, and forms a high, impenetrable hedge that seems to shut out every breath of breeze. Acting on the experiences of the upward march, this portion of the road was now traversed by the troops by night, and consequently heat apoplexy and sunstroke were not encountered. But the string of loaded hammocks grew longer every day!

THE COASTWARD MARCH

On the downward journey the discomforts of the march were added to by the clouds of flies, which up till now had never bothered us; but their presence was only natural, considering the refuse of so large an expedition, which attracted them in spite of every care that was taken to ensure the camp-grounds being kept in clean condition. At every rest-camp an officer and a guard of West Indians had been posted for this work during the expedition, and here one saw something of the thankless jobs that fall to troops on service—and which were, nevertheless, performed with all the zeal and thoroughness that characterised the work in front.

Mansu, Dunkwa, our marching was really coming near its end at last. How eagerly we listened for the first sound of the distant thundering surf, and longed for the first whiff of the sea breeze! And in due course they came. At length, between two hill-tops we saw the grey hazy horizon of the sea, and anon the great white ships all lying ready to take us home. In one short hour our life seemed changed; out of the dank bush and the shadow of disappointment we had come into the sunshine with hopes of home before us.

Cape Coast Castle lay as usual sweltering in the sun, but redeemed by the sea breeze which

THE DOWNFALL OF PREMPEH

blows with steady regularity during the middle hours of the day, but maddening to the sick with its native clamour, heat, and smells. Never since the last expedition had the town been so full of life and business. First to arrive from the front were the gangs of supply carriers to be paid off. Under the charge of Captain Donovan and his lieutenant of the same name, the army of nigh ten thousand of them marched in in military order, and in two days had all been settled up with, paid, and dismissed to their homes.

Soon after them arrived the levy. We had accomplished the march from Kumassi to Cape Coast in seven days. Immediately on arrival the men handed in their arms and ammunition, and on the following morning were paid up and were marched out of the town by companies on their homeward roads. As has been before described, the levy was formed of contingents from half a dozen different tribes. The Bekwai, Abodom, and Adansi contingents had been discharged *en route* as the regiment passed through their respective countries. The latter, who had chiefly performed the scouting duties, received as "dash" or reward the guns with which they had been provided by Government. This was at Prahsu. They then went on as a guard of honour to the

THE COASTWARD MARCH

remainder of the levy, firing salutes as they went, until the village was reached in which their king resides. The king—a decrepit but loyal old man—came out to receive his men from me, and in his conversation showed his gratitude to the British for getting back for his people their own country about the Adansi hills, and stated it as his intention to return there and re-establish the Adansi capital in its former site at Fommenah. Although the men were glad to get back to their homes, the parting between them and their three white officers was full of regret on both sides, for in the short time they had been enrolled they had already picked up such discipline and drill as had made them a useful and reliable body of men, and it seemed a pity that now, just when they had attained a good standard of efficiency, their services should have to be dispensed with.

There was now a pause in the arrivals at the base for several days, but business was very brisk in the Castle—the business of closing up the accounts of the expedition, checking returned stores, condemning and selling those for which there was no longer any further use. Indeed, hard work had been the order of the day there ever since we had left it to go up-country, and fever had been as obstructive at the base as it had been in the bush,

THE DOWNFALL OF PREMPEH

but by transfer to the hospital ship *Coromandel* those who were affected were the more easily enabled to shake it off, and were, as a rule, soon back at their work again.

Here one was able to see something of the English newspapers, and thus to learn something —in addition to the general news of Europe and the world at large—of what we ourselves had been doing in Ashanti. It is a notable fact that, with camps spread about as ours were over a large tract of country, one does not gather all the news that is going, and accompanied as the expedition has been by correspondents of every class and variety, it was natural to find the news was often served up in astonishing and entirely novel form. The departure of one officer from the coast to the next depot at Mansu was headed "A Plucky Dash into the Interior"; hut-building, we are told, was much interfered with by the presence of "serpents"; an illustrated paper gave views of the troops landing at the back of the Castle, where no landing is possible; another showed us Prempeh surrounded by camels and horses, animals unknown at Kumassi, and so on *ad infinitum*; and doubtless we have yet to hear more of the personal feelings of some of those gentlemen who have reason to believe that they have not been

EMBARKATION OF KING PREMPEH

THE COASTWARD MARCH

treated with the respect due to their merit as word-painters. To "those who know" it should be amusing reading.

Soon after daybreak on February 5, the West Yorkshire Regiment marched into the town from Dunkwa, having in their midst King Prempeh and the captive queen and chiefs. These were marched directly to the beach, where eight large surf-boats were lying ready for their embarkation. A few marines and Houssas were posted in each boat to act as escort and to ensure the safety of the prisoners, for it was considered possible that the Kroo boatmen might, in the excess of their hate, contrive to upset Prempeh in the surf, and hold him down till dead! However, all went well. The boats were quickly paddled through the surf, looking, with their paddles, — six a side, — like beetles crawling over crumpled satin, and ere long the prisoners had been transferred aboard H.M.S. *Racoon*. This was to them the climax of their troubles. Awed and nervous at their first sight of the ocean and their first experience of boats and ships, at the utter breaking up of all their royal prestige, and their ignorance of what it might portend, they huddled all together, chiefs and attendants, in one close, frightened group; and presently, as the ship steamed out, their trials

THE DOWNFALL OF PREMPEH

were increased by sea-sickness. An hour's run along the coast brought them abreast of Elmina Fort, and here, much to their relief, the surf-boats took them off and landed them at their final destination.

A harsh, unpromising place it looked to European eyes—a grim, white fort on the surf-lashed strand, whose inner court, which forms the prison, is not inaptly termed the "Bear-pit." Here will Prempeh and his chiefs remain; but attended as they are by a fair allowance of wives and slaves, and with all their wants supplied, their confinement will in no way be a hardship to them. Before Prempeh had reached his prison-house, his late escort, the West Yorkshire Regiment, were already installed on board the transport *Manila*—such of them as were well, but a long string of sick was sent aboard the *Coromandel*. So many that, the following day, when the Special Service Corps arrived, they had to divide the regiment between the two ships for conveyance home, and local steamers called up from neighbouring ports by telegraph were utilised to carry drafts of officers and men according to their various capacities. The bearer company embarked on the *Manila* ere she sailed on the 6th. The immediate headquarter staff are on the *Coromandel*. To-day the

THE COASTWARD MARCH

last of the sick from the base hospital at Conor's Hill have been swung on board: a sick-roll of close on 20 officers and 200 men. Of these nearly all are fever cases, the balance being dysentery; and it is curious to note that the percentage of sick among the officers is greater than that among the men. It is a sight to sadden any eyes to see these pale, limp forms who, but a few weeks back, were men selected for their vigour and robustness to join the expedition.

But the medical arrangements all along the line have been faultless, and have worked without a hitch. Medical attendance and stores have been abundant, sick transport has been carried out with comfort and rapidity, and once on board the hospital ship, with its comfortable, airy wards and its excellent service of hospital orderlies and nursing sisters, the invalids have every chance of speedy recovery. And perhaps the best medicine to the majority of them will be the sound of the screw and the rushing of the seething waters as we steam away out of the "smokes" that envelope this pestilential coast with their noxious haze.

XVI

Homeward Bound

Las Palmas, 16*th February.*

So long as the water supply runs well, the plumber is not thought of. The expedition to Ashanti, having succeeded without hitch or hindrance, one is apt to lose sight of the difficulties that were quietly overcome in its prosecution, and of the important results of its consummation ; whereas, had the preparations been a little less complete in their character, these difficulties would have been more apparent, and disasters possible, and, perhaps, even greater credit would have redounded in the end to those charged with the conduct of the whole. As a matter of fact, this expedition now stands among the many small expeditions of late years as a pattern one for punctuality and rapidity of progress. To these points its success was entirely due, and they were the result only of careful

HOMEWARD BOUND

preparation and thorough organisation. And though every branch distinguished itself by playing its part in a manner as nearly as possible approaching to perfection, the following services have without doubt scored for themselves a record performance — namely, the Transport, Supply, Medical, Telegraph, and Special Service Corps.

The Transport organised in a very few days, one might almost say hours, a larger force of human transport than has before been attempted, and its working has from the first been as eminently satisfactory as it has been vitally necessary to the progress of the expedition. The Supply, ordnance as well as commissariat, has similarly been an unqualified success. Abundance of stores, of the right kind, have been available from first to last at every stage of the operations. Nothing seems to have been forgotten, and nothing superfluous or useless seems to have been brought, which is no small triumph where some 14,000 men of most varied nationalities and requirements had to be catered for, in a land whose products consisted of a very meagre supply of plantains. The medical arrangements were as complete and efficient as could be devised: medical officers and sick hammocks distributed among the corps, bearer company for transport

THE DOWNFALL OF PREMPEH

of sick and wounded, field hospital close up, hammock train laid in, relieving posts for rapid transport of sick to the coast, excellent base hospital at Cape Coast Castle, with sea transport to the capacious and well-equipped hospital ship the *Coromandel.* The Field Telegraph was an unqualified success. It was laid with surprising rapidity, and thus permitted the advanced force to be within rapid communication with headquarters during the whole of the advance to Kumassi. The Special Service Corps—the object of much criticism in England—gained a reputation for itself that must have caused the liveliest satisfaction to the hearts of its supporters. Its small tactical units were eminently suited to the work on hand; the care which had been exercised in the selection of its men as possessing stamina and other qualifications to meet the peculiar conditions of service on the Gold Coast, enabled the corps to maintain its strength and efficiency to a marked extent when contrasted with the ordinary line battalion employed on the same duty; and the emulation of each unit working with all the energy begotten of *esprit de corps* was productive of the best results in practice.

Perhaps one might also add to this record of "records" the fact that the local government

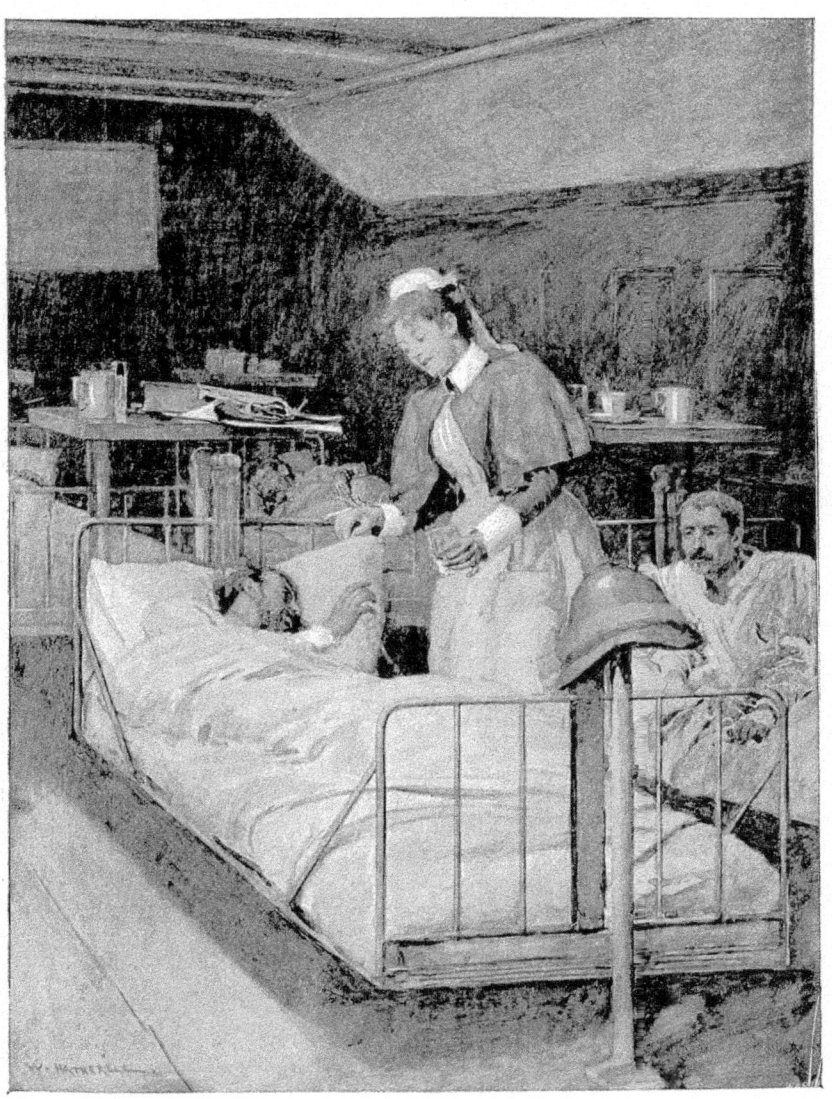

A Ministering Angel
Scene on the Hospital Ship "Coromandel."

HOMEWARD BOUND

worked throughout most effectively and loyally in assisting the expedition. Its employés had already effected much before the head of the expedition proper had even set foot in the colony. The telegraph had been laid—and in a very substantial manner—as far as Mansu; the whole of the material for the bridge over the Prah had been collected at Prahsu, and merely required to be roped for use; the road had been cut and made, and rest-camps set up, from the coast to Prahsu, and the work of collecting natives to act as carriers or native levies had been effected with good results. These were points which an ordinary eye would look at as the natural aim of the local officials, but how seldom do we see them giving their aid in this way, even though the success of an expedition means everything to them. And it must be a source of gratification to many a taxpayer (and I, alas! am one of them) to see that our departments can "run a show" of this kind in a way that transcends anything that has been done in Madagascar, Abyssinia, or Cuba. It is true that it is but a small one, but if your workman "can make a watch, you bet he can make a clock."

With all these organisations thus perfected, the expedition did not, as it could not, fail to succeed;

THE DOWNFALL OF PREMPEH

and yet a few faults in previous preparation, or a very little mismanagement, might have produced a very different result. One need only look to the history of the strip of territory next to Ashanti, namely, Dahomey, or to the late conquest by France in a similar climate against a similar enemy, namely, Madagascar, to see what terrible expense in life and money has been avoided by the use of a well-planned organisation endowed with thorough efficiency in all its working parts.

The secret of the perfection in the preliminary arrangements lies in the fact that most of the heads of the staff at the War Office were themselves employed in the previous campaign in Ashanti, and have been therefore able to order things in accordance with their own personal experience of the country and climate. And the viciousness of this climate is shown by the fact that, in spite of all the forethought and precautions that were taken, no less than fifty per cent. of the men, and something like eighty per cent. of the officers, were attacked by fever. The practical result of the efficient organisation of the expedition was the "rushing" of the Ashantis. At best the Ashantis are slow to mobilise, and on this occasion they were also doubtful how to act

HOMEWARD BOUND

pending the return from England of the envoys they had sent there, and consequently had till then only partially mobilised their army. Within two hours after the returning envoys had crossed the Prah, on their journey to Kumassi, our advanced force had also crossed and followed close upon their heels. The information given by these envoys to the expectant people in Kumassi was to the effect that the British force had been overrated, and was still a long way off. Armed men were then called up, and a raid was organised against the Bekwais, who showed signs of defection; but before the orders had been fully carried out, the Ansahs arrived with fresh information of the British force of white troops being well on the road, and Bekwai itself was suddenly occupied and prepared for defence by our force on the very day on which the Ashantis were to have attacked it. Additional columns were, at the same time, reported as advancing against the capital from the north and from the south-west. There was consequently panic among the leaders; orders and counter-orders were issued—one day it was to be war, the next day peace. Envoys were sent to meet the troops with orders to make every effort to delay their advance till something could be done. But in vain. The stream of

THE DOWNFALL OF PREMPEH

invasion flowed steadily and rapidly forward. There was nothing for it but to distribute all the treasure and valuables for concealment in different parts of the country till the troublous times were over; and then king and chiefs must satisfy the British with whatever promises they might find necessary, so long as they could induce them to go away again. The whole régime was disorganised by the rapid inroad of the expedition; and the panic of the country reached its climax at the arrest and deportation of Prempeh and his chiefs.

From the foregoing it will have been deduced that the success and bloodless victory of the expedition was due to the rapidity and the completeness of the movements of the force; and that this rapidity was in its turn the result of a thoroughly planned and well-equipped organisation. But then arises the question, *Cui bono?* What is the good of this victory when you have won it? What return is there for the half million that will have been spent upon it?

Inter alia, one may at once point out that it has, at anyrate, put an end to the practice of human sacrifice, which, up till within three months ago, had gone on with all the unchecked force that it had ever enjoyed. Fetish super-

HOMEWARD BOUND

stition has an immense hold on the untutored children of the bush, and tradition and custom decreed that human sacrifice was the best form of propitiation of the fetish demons. Moreover, the men of the country have no kind of diversion or employment beyond very poor hunting and an occasional raid on a neighbouring tribe. Bloodlust, like many another vicious habit, rapidly takes root and grows on a man who is without other occupation. A bloody spectacle was naturally to the Ashantis a most attractive form of amusement, especially as at the same time it satisfied their superstition.

The popularity of human sacrifice was none the less great because it gave a direct impetus to the slave trade. As a rule, the victims of fetish sacrifice were slaves, and the supply had to be kept up to the demand. How great that demand was we may, perhaps, never know, but that it was little short of enormous may be guessed partly from the deposit of skulls and bones about the fetish groves, and partly from the fact that two streets in Kumassi consisted of the houses occupied by the official executioners. The suppression of this abuse has been one result of the expedition, and the disintegration of the Ashanti kingdom into its minor kingdoms will ensure its

THE DOWNFALL OF PREMPEH

non-revival. This alliance of lawless chiefs into a common band, under the direction of the Kumassi king, has hitherto acted like a dam to a reservoir. Within five days' march of Kumassi, to the northward, the poisonous bush country comes to an end, and on beyond there lies the open country, rich and populous, which stretches thence to Timbuctoo. The natural outlet for this country's trade is by the Kumassi road to Cape Coast Castle and the sea. This is the reservoir which the Ashanti dam has kept closed up so long. In breaking down the Ashanti gang we have broken up the dam, and the stream which will now begin to flow should, in the near future, well repay the expenses of the machine with which it has been cut. An encouraging example lies to hand in the colony at Lagos, where, as a direct result of the Jebu campaign, the trade has in a single year leaped up to double what it was before.

The British prestige has, moreover, now extended its effect into the back country among tribes who were hitherto wavering with their future allegiance in the balance, and it may be inferred that they will not delay to come under our protectorate. This in its turn will mean the extension of our boundaries till they touch the

HOMEWARD BOUND

Niger, and will thereby save the Gold Coast Colony from being shut out from up-country trade, as had been threatened, by the junction of the two French forces in Dahomey and in Timbuctoo. Indeed, the colonial party of our friends across the Channel are just beginning to suspect that, using Prempeh as a nail to hang our cloak upon, we have quietly beaten them in the race for the Gold Coast Hinterland—that instead of Dahomey joining hands with the French Soudan, the Gold Coast will ere long have marched its boundary on to that of the Royal Niger Protectorate. In gaining this enlarged territory, we may very probably also gain the assistance of a ready-made force with which to hold it, namely, the army, horse and foot, of Samory.

Thus, in the course of a few weeks, an enormous change has been wrought in the history of this part of Africa, and the vista of a great future has been suddenly opened to the Gold Coast Colony. And yet this great result has been gained by the use of a mere handful of men, and it is only when one realises the magnitude of the result that one sees with something akin to awe how much might have been lost by a little mismanagement or by a single false move.

XVII

THE FORMATION OF A NATIVE LEVY

THERE may be those among my readers who would be glad to receive some information regarding the organisation and work of the levy, and who, on the other hand, have not the leisure or inclination to wade through the foregoing pages in search thereof. To save them this trouble, I have thought it right to append the following brief account, extracted, by the kind permission of the editor, from the *Journal of the Royal United Service Institute* for March 1896:—

"Our frequent little wars in all parts of the globe necessitate continually the raising of native levies, and yet one looks in vain for any book that may give one details of organisation, or even the experiences of previous efforts, and that may serve as a guide to similar work when occasion demands it.

FORMATION OF A NATIVE LEVY

"It is, of course, impossible for any hard and fast organisation to be laid down to suit all cases. For example, to attempt to impose some new form of discipline and tactics on a levy of Zulus or Swazis would be to hamper a people already well-grounded in their own form of warfare; whereas with a levy of less warlike folk, such as the West African Coast tribes, some system has to be arranged by which they may be kept in hand by the few white officers available for commanding them.

"It may, therefore, be of interest to many to learn what were the lines upon which the native levy in the recent campaign in Ashanti was organised, and what was the scope of its work.

"On the arrival of the expedition at Cape Coast Castle, on the 13th December last I was ordered to raise and organise a native levy.

"Fortunately I was given the invaluable assistance of an officer who had already some experience of the country and its people, namely, Captain Graham, D.S.O., 5th Lancers.

"Also, through the kind offices of Captain Donald Stewart, I obtained the services of Chief Andoh of Elmina, who proved himself a most loyal and trustworthy adviser on all points of native custom and character.

THE DOWNFALL OF PREMPEH

"The material at hand for forming the levy consisted of some 300 of the Krobo tribe, under their king, Matikoli, and about 100 of the Mumford tribe, under Chief Brew, The Krobos had in former times distinguished themselves as a comparatively warlike race, and they furnished a satisfactory contingent to the native levies in the last campaign against Ashanti. The Mumfords were merely coast fishermen, splendid in physique, but absolutely useless, as they rather proudly admitted, for anything but sea-fishing. They were fitted with—

'Iron sinews, but hearts of mice.'

"Up country, on the Prah, there were already collected 100 warriors of the Adansi tribe. These warriors had already been armed by the civil Government with 'Dane' guns, that is, long flint-lock trade guns, and supplied with a few kegs of powder and bars of lead for ammunition. A store of these arms was lying ready at Prahsu for arming the remainder of the levy as soon as it should arrive there. Two or three days were required to collect the men at Cape Coast Castle, and it was only by adopting somewhat vigorous methods with the chiefs that this time was not prolonged to a week or more.

FORMATION OF A NATIVE LEVY

"The native was apparently incapable of grasping any idea of punctuality; lying was the natural form of every statement or promise he made; lying was the natural attitude assumed by his body, especially when any work was to be done.

"Moreover, in the present instance, the trade gin of the metropolis had come sweet to the lips of the countryman just called up from his village, and his natural stupidity was thereby rendered doubly dense. One good point about these warriors was their cowardice; the least hint of an intention of backing up an order with force ensured its prompt obedience, but this was a trump card which had to be held up with discretion until the frontier was crossed and desertion had become impossible.

"In the meantime, extreme patience, coupled with firmness, was required; exasperation and a rising gorge had to be smoked or whistled down. (There is nothing like whistling an air when you feel exasperated beyond reclaim.)

"It is a West Coast proverb which says, 'Softly, softly, catchee monkey.' This was suggested jokingly as a suitable motto for the stealthily creeping corps of native scouts, but its spirit soon came to be adopted as a guiding principle in practice in all our dealings and

THE DOWNFALL OF PREMPEH

actions. Its meaning might be construed into 'Don't flurry! Work up to your point quietly and steadily.' In a word, 'Patience!'

"The Krobos and Mumfords had at length been coaxed into assembling by the evening of the 16th, and on the following day they were roughly organised in companies under headmen of their respective villages. They were then supplied with red fezes, paraded for the inspection of His Excellency the Governor, and marched off for the interior.

"The ultimate organisation that was found to be best adapted for all purposes, whether for pioneer work, drill, reconnaissance, or outposts, was the division of each tribe into small companies of from twenty to thirty men each.

"Each tribe was under the orders of its chief, and he, or his orderly, understood English, and acted as the adjutant of his detachment, taking all his instructions from the white officer. Each company was under a 'captain,' assisted by an under-captain.

"No specific duties beyond those of acting as scouts had been assigned to the levy; but as we made our way up country, it became evident that much pioneering work would be necessary, in order to make the road passable for troops

FORMATION OF A NATIVE LEVY

through the dense bush, and to prepare clearings and huts for rest-camps. Therefore, whenever we saw a chance of obtaining tools of any description, we did not fail to avail ourselves of it; but in the end, the quantity and quality of our equipment did not amount to anything very considerable, and it was greatly due to the further system applied to our organisation that the levy was able successfully to carry out the pioneering work which it eventually accomplished. Our tools consisted mainly of matchets (long, heavy knives), naval cutlasses, spades, picks, and a few hatchets and felling-axes.

"The companies were permanently detailed to certain kinds of work; thus, one was charged with the work of building bridges, another with making huts, another with digging the road and draining it where necessary, another with felling timber and log-cutting, and so on; so that every man knew his proper work, and with a few days' practice, became proficient in it. But at first much instruction had to be given in the method of using felling-axes, spades, levers, and in knotting ropes—or rather the substitute for rope, the kind of creeper known as 'monkey-rope.'

"Each 'captain' was made responsible for tools used by his company (and these had to be checked

THE DOWNFALL OF PREMPEH

daily, both before and after work), and also for the presence of all his men during working hours, which, with the exception of two hours' rest for the midday meal, generally lasted from daylight till dusk. It was some time before this idea of responsibility for the working of their men could be instilled into the captains, but once it had been grasped by them, and the system had got into working order, all went smoothly and efficiently, so long as a white officer was at hand to keep the rate of progress up to the mark.

"The practical outcome of the pioneer work of the levy was the cutting of over fifty miles of road beyond the Prah through the bush to Kumassi, the bridging of numberless streams, the corduroying of swamps, and the ramping of numerous giant tree-trunks that lay across the path; and also in the clearance of camp-grounds, erection of huts, and the building of three forts; and, lastly, in a piece of work that was comparatively light and yet of paramount importance, namely, in the clearing of the bush round the palace at Kumassi, which enabled that place to be surrounded, and so prevented Prempeh's intended escape when he was 'wanted.'

"Of course, strong measures had at first to be taken to bring the amount of work up to the

NATIVE LEVY BUILDING A FORT

FORMATION OF A NATIVE LEVY

standard required, and the punishment for non-obedience of orders was supposed to be fining; but the native, unaccustomed to much regular payment of any kind, and totally ignorant of payment in arrear, could not understand the meaning of deductions and stoppages, and their infliction was not carried out; more tangible punishment had to be substituted.

"Rations were not issued to the levy, but in order that they might live without raiding when in strange territory, the men were paid threepence a day, and this sufficed to buy them sufficient yams and plantains to satisfy their wants. In addition to this subsistence, the Krobos, Elminas, and Mumfords also drew, in arrears, daily pay at sixpence a man and eighteenpence for a captain. This was less than the pay of carriers, but more than would be given to levies in any other part of our dominions; for, surely, it would seem the duty of warrior-subjects to turn out when called upon for the defence of their country, as a return for our protectorate over them.

"This latter rule was carried out with part of the levy, namely, the Adansis, Bekwais, and Abodoms, and they worked none the less satisfactorily for it—perhaps all the better, as they

THE DOWNFALL OF PREMPEH

hoped, by good work, to obtain a good 'dash' or reward at the end of the campaign.

"While the main body of the levy had been undergoing organisation and equipment about the Prah, as above described, the Adansi contingent of four companies had been acting as scouts and outposts to the front of the Adansi Hills, three-quarters of the way to Kumassi from the coast.

"They were a wild, uncivilised crew, living entirely in the bush, and therefore well adapted for this particular duty.

"It was only necessary to show them a system to work upon, and they readily grasped it. Briefly, the plan for outpost duties was this: Each company formed a piquet, and during the day it had sentries out for all paths leading to it. These sentries were concealed in the bush close by the path, and within reach of recall by the horn sounding at the piquet. Patrols of two or three men went out for the whole day on every path. No individual work could be got out of natives at night—the bush was too full of fairies and fetish devils for that. Therefore, after dark, instead of the day sentries and patrols, small detached posts of half a dozen men each were bivouacked on every path, at a distance of about a mile from the piquet.

FORMATION OF A NATIVE LEVY

"In addition to their watchfulness, the Adansis, and also the Bekwais and Abodoms (who were afterwards added to them for detached duties), distinguished themselves by their quickness in detecting the presence of an enemy, and by the rapidity with which they conveyed the news not only to their commander, but also to neighbouring piquets and parties.

"Their faculty, too, for finding their way in the forest, whether by day or by night, was surprising. They could not explain it themselves, but, like the forest tribes of South-Eastern Africa, they were in no way guided by sun or stars— some natural instinct brought them through.

"In the meantime, the Krobo portion of the levy had been armed with Snider rifles, and, in the intervals of work and on the march, the companies were instructed by Captain Graham in the use of their arms and in the elements of drill. This instruction chiefly took the form of the principles of the firing exercise, and its practice in action in the bush. A few simple whistle-signals were employed to signify "Halt," "Advance," "Rally," "Cease firing," etc., and these were readily learnt by the men.

"The supply of ammunition was kept up by means of an ammunition carrier to each company.

THE DOWNFALL OF PREMPEH

Every man was allowed five rounds only, loose in his pouch, with another five rounds tied up. This would, it was hoped, do something to check indiscrimate blazing away. Unfortunately, the work told upon Captain Graham, and in the midst of it he was struck down, and for a time incapacitated by fever; and the same fate befell two more officers who were thereupon successively attached to the levy for duty, namely, Captain Williams, South Staffordshire Regiment, and Captain Green, Gold Coast Houssas. Major Gordon, 15th Hussars, then joined us, and would have been an ideal leader for the men had it been our fortune to come to blows with the enemy.

"The levy eventually was composed as follows :—

      8 companies of Krobos,
      2 ,, ,, Mumfords,
      1 company of Elminas,
      4 companies of Adansis,
      2 ,, ,, Bekwais,
      1 company of Abodoms,

having a total strength of 860. Of these eighteen companies, eleven were more or less disciplined, armed with Sniders, and equipped with tools for pioneering. The remaining seven companies

FORMATION OF A NATIVE LEVY

were irregulars, armed with flint-lock guns, and specially useful as scouts and for outpost and reconnaissance work.

"The first actual test of the marching and scouting power of the levy and of its discipline was the march to the assistance of Bekwai. This was carried out by night as well as by day, and in the presence of an outpost and scouts of the enemy. The levy was backed up by two companies of Houssas, and this no doubt helped to give it the confidence it displayed, and which contributed to its rapid and successful completion of the duty.

"After this experience there was no doubt of its ability to work, if not in a bold and dashing manner, at least warily and usefully; and this was borne out in the final advance on Kumassi, when the levy forming the advanced guard was divided into three parties and approached the place by three different routes. The central party on the main road cut the path for the troops. Its covering party being sent to within a short distance of Kumassi, the remainder was distributed in cutting parties at intervals along the track; by this disposition the last six miles of road were cleared in two hours. On arrival at Kumassi the levy formed outposts to cover the arrival of the main

THE DOWNFALL OF PREMPEH

body, and continued to find the outposts all round the camp during the stay of the troops there.

"These outposts were partly employed for the purpose of protecting villagers bringing in supplies to the market, and partly to prevent native followers from going out to raid on their own account, and they were also useful, especially at night, in preventing the escape of Prempeh and his chiefs from Kumassi. It was certainly due to their vigilance that Prempeh did not escape on the night before his arrest.

"The palace had been reconnoitred soon after the arrival of the troops, and we had then found that its garden adjoined the bush at the back, and that a small postern existed in the fence, and led by a footpath through this bush, across the swamp and into the forest beyond.

"The levy therefore went to work with matchets, and in a few hours had cut away a broad, open space all round the palace enclosure; and thus, when the time came, it was found possible to draw a cordon of men rapidly round the place, to prevent not only the escape of its inmates, but also looting parties from gaining an entrance.

"On the night before the arrest the piquets

FORMATION OF A NATIVE LEVY

on all the roads were reinforced, and an extra patrol was stationed to watch what went on at the palace. Messengers from the palace and others were caught trying all the roads, and during the night one of the Ansahs was captured by the piquet on the so-called 'secret' path.

"There had been some difficulty in obtaining information as to where the queen-mother resided, but at three o'clock in the morning the patrol saw her come out of the palace and go to her home in the town, and there they marked her down with a piquet until she might be wanted.

"There is good reason to suppose that the palace party had intended to escape that night, but were obliged to abandon their plan on finding every road stopped.

"The last pioneering task carried out by the levy was the very satisfactory one of levelling the smouldering walls of the burnt fetish houses at Bantama.

"Then part of the levy made a night march and reconnaissance to a place five miles beyond Kumassi, where 400 of Mampon's men were reported to be encamped, but these got wind of our coming, and slipped away; and a reconnaissance the same day to Maheer, the king's summer residence, only arrived there to find that the place

THE DOWNFALL OF PREMPEH

had already been looted by the slaves left in charge of it.

"Next came the march down to the coast with all the royal and other prisoners. The part taken by the levies in the early portion of this march was not an unimportant one, since to them fell the duty of searching the bush, and of holding all by-roads, to guard against attempts which we had reason to expect would be made to assassinate Prempeh. They found numbers of individual men in the bush, but these always came in asking for news, and were evidently runaway slaves rather than would-be assassins.

"On the 22nd January the levy marched out of Kumassi; on the 29th it arrived at Cape Coast Castle, thus completing a march of 150 miles in seven days, which in that climate is not a bad performance.

"This brief *résumé* of the work done by the levy will tend to show to what extent it was capable of being useful in the short period of its enrolment, after being organised on the principles above stated.

"It is not claimed that such organisations could also go so far as to put pluck into the men, but it is only reasonable to infer that if they had been brought into actual conflict with the Ashantis, they

EXAMINING A PRISONER

Page 176

FORMATION OF A NATIVE LEVY

would at least have shown themselves no worse than their enemy; they would at anyrate have been perfectly under control of their officers; and they would probably have been emboldened to a very useful extent by the possession of better arms, and by their superiority in tactical power.

"A reliable authority on the subject has stated that, in his opinion, West African tribes are worse than useless as levies, for two reasons: one is that their natural cowardice will lead them, when the fight is going against them, to run away at the critical moment, and in their panic in the narrow bush path to overrun and bear back with them the steadier troops in support; the other is that in a winning fight their want of discipline will, on the other hand, lead them to commit excesses such as would be unbecoming in allies of the British.

"But in dealing with a native levy in any part of the world, one or other of these difficulties, often both, will have to be encountered by the white commander; and the sooner he realises that other means must of necessity be used for enforcing discipline than ordinary commands or requests, the sooner he will find himself properly obeyed. These have to be resorted to occasionally as the lesser of evils, up to the point of shooting one's

THE DOWNFALL OF PREMPEH

own men; but when resorted to they should be the result only of deliberate and fair consideration of the case. Strict justice goes a very long way towards bringing natives under discipline. A very few lessons suffice, as a rule, to show them that an order is not to be trifled with; and once this idea has been ingrafted into their minds, they become very amenable to discipline.

"In the late Ashanti expedition, although we had no fighting to do, the pioneering, scouting, and outpost work performed by the native levy were sufficiently valuable in their results to justify very fully its enrolment, in spite of the fact that it was composed of the much-abused West Coast tribes."

POLICY AND WEALTH IN ASHANTI, 1895

POLICY AND WEALTH IN ASHANTI, 1895
By Sir George Baden-Powell

———◆———

In 1895-96 we wage the fourth serious Ashanti war within half a century. The cost in blood and treasure, in valuable lives, felt so heavily by the august head of the nation, as well as by the nation at large, and in valued money, should be a very special concern to the representatives of the people. The ultimate unit, the tax-payer,—whether home or colonial,—looks for two groups of results as his reward. On the one hand, he hopes to see Christianity and civilisation *pro tanto* extended; and, on the other, to see some compensating development of industry and trade. Unless he, or "his servants the Government," secure either or both these results, the question must be plainly asked, has he the right, and is he right, to wage such wars? In relation to Ashanti,

THE DOWNFALL OF PREMPEH

the solution of this problem in politics has a very present and direct importance, as well as an indirect and more general significance.

First of all, the place in history of Ashanti as it stands to-day is remarkable. The "Gold Coast" was the one part of the African coast which attracted the earliest navigators of Western Europe, because of its gold.

The very first English traders—Windham, Lok, Hawkins, and others—visited Guinea for gold. This legitimate commercial adventure was, however, promptly superseded by another and even more profitable trade, namely, that in slaves. The one crying need of the gold mines and plantations, which European enterprise was just then opening up in tropical America,—in the West Indies, in Mexico, in Peru, in Brazil,—was black labour. From the days of the Greeks and Romans right down to modern times, Africa was the one great slave preserve; and to Africa came the Europeans to filch that human labour they so much needed in the New World. The trade speedily assumed enormous proportions, and overwhelmed all other forms of enterprise and commerce. The very lowest traits of the native races were thereby cultivated, and the most ruinous of all industries was developed. The

POLICY AND WEALTH IN ASHANTI

south-east and the north-east trade-winds competed, as it were, to waft from Africa to America these human cargoes; and the heavy blight of the slave trade hung over Africa and over all attempts at European settlement or civilisation from the sixteenth to the middle of the nineteenth century. All along that portion of the coast of Guinea which runs eastward from Cape Palmas to the Delta of the Niger, 1000 miles in length, where the natives brought down gold and ivory as well as slaves, European forts and factories were established from the earliest times.

But, confining ourselves to the present century, we come to the period referred to by Mr. C. P. Lucas in his most admirable *Historical Geography of the British Colonies* (vol. iii. p. 117):

"The English went for generations to Africa to follow up the slave trade. Then they went again to put it down."

The putting an end suddenly to this great and vigorous trade burdened the nation with the responsibilities of the slave-trading merchants. Their forts and factories and settlements at once fell to the ultimate charge of the Home Government, and for the succeeding fifty years we see the British Government, with the steady vacilla-

THE DOWNFALL OF PREMPEH

tion of a pendulum, alternately taking over administration from and handing it back to the traders.

Early in this century the Government found Cape Coast Castle itself to be rented from the Fantis. But the Ashantis were attacking the coast tribes, and setting up a very effective suzerainty, and claiming all rents and tributes; nor did they hesitate boldly to attack the whites.

In 1816 the Ashantis actually blockaded Cape Coast Castle, and in the following year the traders sent an embassy to Kumassi, where they made a convention recognising the suzerainty of the Ashantis, but stipulating for a British Resident at Kumassi. The following year the Home Government sent an embassy to Kumassi, and there was great friction between the Government and the merchants on the coast. The Ashantis, hoping to profit by these dissensions, made a formidable invasion of the small British territories in 1821.

In 1824 came the *first* Ashanti war. Sir Charles M'Carthy led a British force, chiefly composed of native troops, across the Prah. But the force was completely demolished, and he himself slain. The consequence was a fresh Ashanti

POLICY AND WEALTH IN ASHANTI

invasion, and they were only beaten off in their attack on Accra by means of the newly introduced war-rockets, which are said to have had a widely-spread effect among the natives, who took them to be lightning and thunder in the hands of the white men. In 1831 followed a treaty freeing all the forts from Ashanti suzerainty. At this period Governor Maclean, under the rule of the merchants, established a quasi-British authority along a great stretch of coast, and set up sovereign claims. He maintained unbroken peace with the Ashantis.

In 1840 the Home Government once again took complete charge of the Gold Coast, and after this commenced the policy of buying out the smaller Dutch and Danish possessions.

In 1863 another attempt at armed interference with Ashanti took place. The *second* invasion was made; but the result was a terrible military disaster, chiefly due to the undertaking of operations at the wrong season, and the consequent abandonment of the expedition owing to the terrible ravages of sickness among the troops.

The trend of opinion in England at this moment was against the widening responsibilities of empire, and in 1865 the House of Commons adopted the notorious resolution of withdrawal

THE DOWNFALL OF PREMPEH

from the West Coast of Africa, in which it was declared: "All further extension of territory or assumption of government or new treaties offering any protection to native tribes would be inexpedient . . . with a view to ultimate withdrawal from all (West African possessions) except, probably, Sierra Leone."

But this "Little Englander" resolution proved mere waste paper in the face of the actual work in process on the West Coast. As a matter of fact, the purchasing of the smaller foreign settlements marked a great consolidation and strengthening of the British power at the very moment when the self-sufficient representatives of the people were passing their most impracticable and impossible academic resolution.

But this first consolidation of British power twenty-five years ago on the Gold Coast found the powerful Ashanti nation—one versed in all the worst forms and practices of fetish and barbaric tyranny—closely hemming in all our settlements and small protectorates. Some great conflict between the two powers became inevitable.

In 1873 occurred the *third* Ashanti war. When Sir Garnet Wolseley arrived at Cape Coast Castle, he found the Ashanti forces at its very

POLICY AND WEALTH IN ASHANTI

gates. Commodore Commerell had been seriously wounded by an Ashanti ambush at the very mouth of the Prah; and Sir Garnet fought his first pitched battle with the enemy at Abrakampa, not eight miles from Cape Coast Castle.

Thus 25 years ago on the Gold Coast the Queen's authority barely extended outside the forts and factories established 250 years before.

But the results of the Wolseley Ashanti war were very significant. By a series of brilliant actions and marches, Sir Garnet very speedily captured the Ashanti capital, and dictated terms to the king. The military work done was all that could be desired: the political action which followed was the very reverse. We had seized and occupied the fountainhead of Ashanti barbarism; we had it in our power completely and finally to purify the whole stream of Ashanti influence. Instead of this we retired, imagining, in our folly, that a nation steeped to the lips in barbarism and savagery would abide by and carry out the terms of a paper convention.

The consequences of our folly developed rapidly and surely, and in twenty years came to disastrous fruition. Every vice, every evil, every terror known to savagery came to be rampant over all Ashanti. The main clauses of the convention—

THE DOWNFALL OF PREMPEH

the war indemnity, the abolition of human sacrifices, the keeping open of the roads, and the freeing of trade and traffic—remained a dead letter.

Thus, in defence of the interests of our own colony and of numerous natives, we were compelled once again to use force, and enter upon the *fourth* Ashanti war.

The one permanent gain due to the 1873 campaign was that the British frontier was carried up to and across the Prah river.

But the whole of the area behind our own possessions, with a boundary running by the Hinterland of the new German acquisitions in Togoland, past the eastern ends of French Guinea and the French Soudan, round by the borders of the Niger Company's territories, down to the frontiers of the new French possessions in Dahomey—all that area, where not overrun by the mysterious Moslem forces headed by "Samory," was in 1895 under the domination of the Ashanti king, Prempeh.

His rule involved all the insecurity inevitable to active slave-raiding; all the cruel misery and drain of population incidental to the system of wholesale human sacrifices; all the destitution and retrogression due to ruthless repression of

POLICY AND WEALTH IN ASHANTI

industry by the ruling powers; no profits of industry or trade were safe; no man could be sure of reaping what he sowed, or of retaining the price he obtained for the wild but valuable products of the forest. All gold found or obtained by any form of work had to be delivered up to the chief or king. All was stagnation, poverty, and cruelty.

The mere putting an end to such a state of affairs would be even a noble reason for conquest by force of arms. And when, for the other reasons of broken treaty-pledges and the material damage done to our own interests and to those of the natives for whom we had become responsible, armed interference on our part became necessary, then those among us who had watched such affairs recognised a grand opportunity for doing a great and good act on the part of the British power.

In 1823 we sacrificed the lives of our own men and the lives of the enemy without securing any good in return for so much evil.

In 1863, again, we sacrifice 1000 lives on our own side and untold numbers of the foe, but no permanent good results follow.

In 1873 once again we embark on a campaign against the same Ashantis, at a human sacrifice

THE DOWNFALL OF PREMPEH

to ourselves of 300 killed and wounded and an untold loss to the enemy.

Each time we press our frontier a little forward. But, to the disgrace of our statesmen, each time, even this last time in 1873, we retire from and surrender to the despotism of savagery all the area of Ashanti proper; and in so far make our own country responsible for all the fetish practices, the human sacrifices, the slave raiding, and other such curses, which have brooded over that land and its unfortunate inhabitants for the past quarter of a century.

Here, again, as in many another instance, the philanthropy of the British nation has seen and judged aright of the evils of such barbaric despotism, and has set itself, regardless of cost, to crush such despotism. But here again, as in so many other instances, the statesmen in office, as a rule through craven fear of electioneering results, have ignored the further moral obligation of setting up some better power in the stead of that which we have destroyed.

As in Zululand in 1881, so in Ashanti in 1873, we crushed a great native organisation and retired, setting up nothing in its place. The invariable consequences follow, namely, a recrudescence and intensification of previous cruelties and barbarities,

POLICY AND WEALTH IN ASHANTI

further dishonour to the national credit, and ultimately fresh expense, fresh expeditions, and fresh human sacrifices in war.

Such must not be permitted to be the result of the 1895-96 expedition. We are bound in honour to the natives to provide them with some better form of government than that from which we have saved them by force of arms. We have crushed the barbaric despotism, but we have yet to make our conquest over the demoralising agencies of slavery, savagery, and drunkenness. We have yet definitely to set up the Queen's peace over all this new area; yet definitely to establish law, order, and security. And to accomplish these ends, all we have to do is to *administer*. The means to this end are elastic, and must be suited to the special circumstances of each district and date. The whole area must at once be divided into provisional districts, and a white chief placed over each. Armed support each must have, and white assistants, as many as he needs, be always available. Gradually must be instilled the leading ideas of our civilisation—the sanctity of private property; individual liberty; security for person and property, and so forth. There are instruments to this end to be found in native courts armed police, legitimate revenue-raising, and so forth.

THE DOWNFALL OF PREMPEH

Another side to the political aspect must be at once taken in hand. We must cultivate the most friendly relations with the independent powers bordering on this our province,—with the German and French colonies on either side, and with the daring and independent chief "Samory" at the back,—and with them not only make mutual and final demarcations of frontier, but also institute such combined arrangements as shall prohibit and prevent the deleterious trades in spirits, arms, and ammunition, and all other infringements of the salutary ordinances of civilised authority.

Such is the policy of honour we must pursue; and it is the policy of common sense as well.

Over this Ashanti area, which now comes definitely under our flag, there exists, according to indisputable evidence, abundance of wealth, mineral, vegetable, and animal. The following records of exports indicate what has occurred before and after our Gold Coast Colony spread its administrative ægis as far as the Prah, and this will give some indication of results in progress and prosperity which the spread of British jurisdiction can bring over all the Hinterland of that colony:—

POLICY AND WEALTH IN ASHANTI

Exports from the Gold Coast Colony.

	1882.	1892.
Palm oil	£179,000	£179,000
Palm kernels	50,000	134,000
Rubber	...	137,000
Monkey skins	4,000	35,000
Gold	62,000	99,000
	£295,000	£584,000

The value of the colony as a new market for British produce is seen by remarking that ten years ago the imports were less than £300,000, and now they are close upon £600,000.

But the figures of actual trade hardly indicate what is the main feature in the wealth of an expanding colony, and that is the corresponding power of the expansion of trade. The following table gives at a glance the records of expansion at twenty-year periods of the Gold Coast Colony:—

	1853.	1873.	1893.
Area (square miles)	6,000	29,000	39,000
Population	150,000	410,000	1,474,000
Tonnage	36,000	180,000	831,000
Imports	£60,000	£360,000	£718,000
Exports	£125,000	£321,000	£722,000
Index numbers	43	130	408

THE DOWNFALL OF PREMPEH

In rough result this colony, which nearly trebled its commercial value in the twenty years preceding 1873, has nearly quadrupled its commercial value in the last twenty years, and three-fourths of the total trade is with the United Kingdom.

But this new province has as yet had no more exploiting than a "mere scratching of the earth." In all the staples there has been no systematised production as yet. We have indications of many minor products of value, such as grain, ivory, quicksilver, and petroleum. But in regard to the staples, much remains to be done before this area can be said to be producing anything like its legitimate output.

Take *gold*, for instance. As I have said, hitherto the chief or king took all the gold that was found—a far heavier levy even than that of the English Crown on the gold miners in Wales. And yet there are indications in numerous old works; and, above all, in the undoubted fact that natural nuggets, indicating alluvial gold deposits, abound among the native hoards, that we have not yet got hold, in any appreciable degree, of the natural stores of the precious metal which gives its name to all the coast.

One word more as to gold. It has often been a fact of history that the value of the output of

POLICY AND WEALTH IN ASHANTI

gold in a given country has not exceeded the cost, that, in some cases, the gold obtained at a total cost of £5 the ounce, has, of course, fetched in the market only £3, 17s. 6d. And yet the district or country prospered exceedingly. The fact is, that the raising of gold means considerable success to a great many incomers. It also means considerable loss by means of considerable expenditure to a great many others. But it means in the aggregate the coming into the district of the successful and the unsuccessful, and the expenditure there of much wealth by both classes. The consequence is, a great many other industries spring up, and many hitherto unnoticed local resources become developed.

It is the same with other industries, as, for instance, that of timber-getting; and it is certain that portions of the Ashanti forests consist of valuable African mahogany.

A word must be said on the modern method of discovering and developing the unknown resources of such a country. This is nowadays done by means of concessions from the Government. In regard to these, the very first point is to discover that any particular concession is obtained fairly and squarely; and the second point is to see that the financial arrangements are equitable.

THE DOWNFALL OF PREMPEH

The most modern proposal is, that the Government should only grant concessions for which large sums are paid, which the Government undertakes shall be expended in the public works necessary for the carrying out of the concession, such as roads, bridges, railways, telegraphs, and water supply. But in making such stipulations it would be foolish and wrong on the part of the Government to insist on too high a price for concessions. In untried and unknown countries the development of any industry is carried on at considerable and unknown risk, and the commercial value of an untried concession must be calculated with due consideration of these unknown risks, and a balance struck by prospectively large profits. In short, as large a margin of possible profit must be left to the investor, or he will not face the possible losses. Nor should he alone be saddled with expenses, such as those of providing improved means of communication, which necessarily benefit so large an area of country and so many other persons.

With an official policy of development, based on sound financial principles, and controlled by adequate knowledge of such countries, there should be no difficulty in securing the rapid industrial opening up of all Ashanti.

POLICY AND WEALTH IN ASHANTI

In two matters, however, the Government must take action forthwith. A light railway must at once be constructed to the Prah, with a view to ultimate extension right into the Hinterland; and a sufficient breakwater must be built, probably at Accra, to render easier the landing and shipping of goods.

In this work of the political and industrial regeneration of Ashanti, the missionaries, to say nothing here of their immediate and great religious work, do give invaluable aid. They are, as they have been before, ready to establish stations at all available centres over the interior, and thus to set up the standard of Christian and civilised lives for all men to look at. And they become, as they are already in the more settled districts, invaluable in all matters connected with the education of the natives.

As is proved by the recorded results in all other cases, thus to set up the British idea and British administration over all this great new area is bound very speedily to yield handsome returns in commerce and finance, to the great advantage, not only of the traders and shipowners already engaged, but also to the exporters and manufacturers of the mother country. It is no mean advantage to them to discover, even in Ashanti, a new market which,

THE DOWNFALL OF PREMPEH

if properly organised, should take in a few years probably from two to three million pounds worth of British produce each year.

Moreover, in thus setting up strongly and definitely the Queen's peace over this great native area, in the place of the degrading, demoralising, and pauperising régime hitherto dominant, we shall be bringing to perhaps four or five millions of natives all the advantages of peaceful industry and commerce, and teach them, in the most practical manner, the benefits of attaching themselves to a civilisation which, as they will then very speedily come to see, has its roots in those high principles of law, order, justice, and goodwill for all men, which are, after all, the guiding lessons taught by our firm national religion.

The nation, therefore, has good cause, whether from the religious, the philanthropic, the financial, or the commercial point of view, for very great gratitude to those who, at great risk of life and health, have so signally and speedily crushed the opposing barbaric forces which stood in the way of a wholesome and profitable regeneration of all Ashanti.

In Ashanti the British nation can now do a piece of work of inestimable material benefit to

POLICY AND WEALTH IN ASHANTI

themselves and to the natives, and which can become an invaluable object lesson both for ourselves and for foreign nations, in the extension to tropical areas of the benefits of Christianity and civilisation.

GEORGE BADEN-POWELL.

A CATALOGUE OF BOOKS AND ANNOUNCEMENTS OF METHUEN AND COMPANY PUBLISHERS : LONDON 36 ESSEX STREET W.C.

CONTENTS

	PAGE
FORTHCOMING BOOKS,	2
POETRY,	8
BELLES LETTRES,	9
ILLUSTRATED BOOKS,	11
HISTORY,	12
BIOGRAPHY,	14
TRAVEL, ADVENTURE AND TOPOGRAPHY,	15
NAVAL AND MILITARY,	17
GENERAL LITERATURE,	18
SCIENCE,	19
TECHNOLOGY,	20
PHILOSOPHY,	20
THEOLOGY,	21
FICTION,	23
BOOKS FOR BOYS AND GIRLS,	34
THE PEACOCK LIBRARY,	34
UNIVERSITY EXTENSION SERIES,	35
SOCIAL QUESTIONS OF TO-DAY	36
CLASSICAL TRANSLATIONS	37
EDUCATIONAL BOOKS,	37

FEBRUARY 1898

FEBRUARY 1898.

MESSRS. METHUEN'S ANNOUNCEMENTS

Poetry

THE POEMS OF WILLIAM SHAKESPEARE. Edited with an Introduction and Notes by GEORGE WYNDHAM, M.P. *Demy 8vo. Buckram, gilt top.* 10s. 6d.

This edition contains the 'Venus,' 'Lucrece' and Sonnets, and is prefaced with an elaborate introduction of over 140 pp. The text is founded on the first quartos, with an endeavour to retain the original reading. A set of notes deals with the problems of Date, The Rival Poets, Typography, and Punctuation; and the editor has commented on obscure passages in the light of contemporary works. The publishers believe that no such complete edition has ever been published.

Travel and Adventure

THREE YEARS IN SAVAGE AFRICA. By LIONEL DECLE. With an Introduction by H. M. STANLEY, M.P. With 100 Illustrations and 5 Maps. *Demy 8vo.* 21s.

Few Europeans have had the same opportunity of studying the barbarous parts of Africa as Mr. Decle. Starting from the Cape, he visited in succession Bechuanaland, the Zambesi, Matabeleland and Mashonaland, the Portuguese settlement on the Zambesi, Nyasaland, Ujiji, the headquarters of the Arabs, German East Africa, Uganda (where he saw fighting in company with the late Major 'Roddy' Owen), and British East Africa. In his book he relates his experiences, his minute observations of native habits and customs, and his views as to the work done in Africa by the various European Governments, whose operations he was able to study. The whole journey extended over 7000 miles, and occupied exactly three years.

EXPLORATION AND HUNTING IN CENTRAL AFRICA. By Major A. ST. H. GIBBONS, F.R.G.S. With 8 fullpage Illustrations by C. WHYMPER, photographs and Map. *Demy 8vo.* 15s.

This is an account of travel and adventure among the Marotse and contiguous tribes, with a description of their customs, characteristics, and history, together with the author's experiences in hunting big game. The illustrations are by Mr. Charles Whymper, and from photographs. There is a map by the author of the hitherto unexplored regions lying between the Zambezi and Kafukwi rivers and from 18° to 15° S. lat.

WITH THE MASHONALAND FIELD FORCE, 1896. By Lieut.-Colonel ALDERSON. With numerous Illustrations and Plans. *Demy 8vo.* 12s. 6d.

This is an account of the military operations in Mashonaland by the officer who commanded the troops in that district during the late rebellion. Besides its interest as a story of warfare, it will have a peculiar value as an account of the services of mounted infantry by one of the chief authorities on the subject.

Messrs. Methuen's Announcements

CAMPAIGNING ON THE UPPER NILE AND NIGER. By Lieut. SEYMOUR VANDELEUR. With an Introduction by Sir G. GOLDIE. With two Maps, Illustrations and Plans. *Large Cr. 8vo.* 10s. 6d.

A narrative of service (1) in the Equatorial Lakes and on the Upper Nile in 1895 and 1896; and (2) under Sir George Goldie in the Niger campaign of January 1897, describing the capture of Bida and Ilorin, and the French occupation of Boussa. The book thus deals with the two districts of Africa where now the French and English stand face to face.

THE NIGER SOURCES. By Colonel J. TROTTER, R.A. With a Map and Illustrations. *Crown 8vo.* 5s.

A book which at the present time should be of considerable interest, being an account of a Commission appointed for frontier delimitation.

LIFE AND PROGRESS IN AUSTRALASIA. By MICHAEL DAVITT, M.P. With two Maps. *Crown 8vo.* 6s. 500 pp.

This book, the outcome of a recent journey through the seven Australasian colonies, is an attempt to give to English readers a more intimate knowledge of a continent colonised by their own race. The author sketches the general life, resources, politics, parties, progress, prospects, and scenery of each colony. He made a careful examination of the West Australian goldfields, and he has paid special attention to the development of practical politics in the colonies. The book is full of anecdotes and picturesque description.

History and Biography

A HISTORY OF THE ART OF WAR. By C. W. OMAN, M.A., Fellow of All Souls', Oxford. Vol. II. MEDIÆVAL WARFARE. *Demy 8vo. Illustrated.* 21s.

Mr. Oman is engaged on a History of the Art of War, of which the above, though covering the middle period from the fall of the Roman Empire to the general use of gunpowder in Western Europe, is the first instalment. The first battle dealt with will be Adrianople (378) and the last Navarette (1367). There will appear later a volume dealing with the Art of War among the Ancients, and another covering the 15th, 16th, and 17th centuries.

The book will deal mainly with tactics and strategy, fortifications and siegecraft, but subsidiary chapters will give some account of the development of arms and armour, and of the various forms of military organization known to the Middle Ages.

RELIGION AND CONSCIENCE IN ANCIENT EGYPT. By W. M. FLINDERS PETRIE, D.C.L., LL.D. *Fully Illustrated. Crown 8vo.* 2s. 6d.

This volume deals mainly with the historical growth of the Egyptian religion, and the arrangement of all the moral sayings into something like a handbook. But far larger interests are also discussed as the origin of intolerance, the fusion of religions, the nature of conscience, and the experimental illustration of British conscience.

SYRIA AND EGYPT FROM THE TELL EL AMARNA TABLETS. By W. M. FLINDERS PETRIE, D.C.L., LL.D. *Crown 8vo.* 2s. 6d.

This book describes the results of recent researches and discoveries and the light thereby thrown on Egyptian history.

4 MESSRS. METHUEN'S ANNOUNCEMENTS

THE DECLINE AND FALL OF THE ROMAN EMPIRE.
By EDWARD GIBBON. A New Edition, edited with Notes, Appendices, and Maps by J. B. BURY, M.A., Fellow of Trinity College, Dublin. *In Seven Volumes. Demy 8vo, gilt top.* 8s. 6d. each. *Crown 8vo.* 6s. each. *Vol. V.*

THE EASTERN QUESTION IN THE EIGHTEENTH CENTURY. By ALBERT SOREL of the French Academy. Translated by F. C. BRAMWELL, M.A., with an Introduction by R. C. L. FLETCHER, Fellow of Magdalen College, Oxford. With a Map. *Crown 8vo.* 4s. 6d.

This book is a study of the political conditions which led up to and governed the first partition of Poland, and the Russo-Turkish war of 1768-1774. It is probably the best existing examination of Eastern European politics in the eighteenth century, and is an early work of one of the ablest of living historians.

THE LETTERS OF VICTOR HUGO. Translated from the French by F. CLARKE, M.A. *In Two Volumes. Demy 8vo.* 10s. 6d. each. *Vol. II.* 1815-35.

A HISTORY OF THE GREAT NORTHERN RAILWAY, 1845-95. By C. H. GRINLING. With Maps and many Illustrations. *Demy 8vo.* 10s. 6d.

A record of Railway enterprise and development in Northern England, containing much matter hitherto unpublished. It appeals both to the general reader and to those specially interested in railway construction and management.

ANARCHISM. By E. V. ZENKER. *Demy 8vo.* 7s. 6d.

A critical study and history, as well as trenchant criticism of the Anarchist movement in Europe. The book has aroused considerable attention on the Continent.

THOMAS CRANMER. By A. J. MASON, D.D., Canon of Canterbury. With a Portrait. *Crown 8vo.* 3s. 6d.

[*Leaders of Religion.*

Theology

THE MINISTRY OF DEACONESSES. By CECILIA ROBINSON, Deaconess. With an Introduction by the LORD BISHOP OF WINCHESTER, and an Appendix by Professor ARMITAGE ROBINSON. *Crown 8vo.* 3s. 6d.

This book is a review of the history and theory of the office and work of a Deaconess and it may be regarded as authoritative.

DISCIPLINE AND LAW. By H. HENSLEY HENSON, B.D., Fellow of All Soul's, Oxford; Incumbent of St. Mary's Hospital, Ilford; Chaplain to the Bishop of St. Albans. *Fcap. 8vo.* 2s. 6d.

This volume of devotional addresses, suitable for Lent, is concerned with the value, method, and reward of Discipline; and with Law—family, social and individual.

REASONABLE CHRISTIANITY. By HASTINGS RASHDALL, M.A., Fellow and Tutor of New College, Oxford. *Crown 8vo.* 6s

This volume consists of twenty sermons, preached chiefly before the University of Oxford. They are an attempt to translate into the language of modern thought some of the leading ideas of Christian theology and ethics.

Messrs. Methuen's Announcements

THE HOLY SACRIFICE. By F. WESTON, M.A., Curate of St. Matthew's, Westminster. *Pott 8vo.* 1s.

A small volume of devotions at the Holy Communion, especially adapted to the needs of servers and of those who do not communicate.

The Churchman's Library.

Edited by J. H. BURN, B.D.

A series of books by competent scholars on Church History, Institutions, and Doctrine, for the use of clerical and lay readers.

THE BEGINNINGS OF ENGLISH CHRISTIANITY. By W. E. COLLINS, M.A., Professor of Ecclesiastical History at King's College, London. With Map. *Crown 8vo.* 3s. 6d.

An investigation in detail, based upon original authorities, of the beginnings of the English Church, with a careful account of earlier Celtic Christianity. The larger aspects of the continental movement are described, and some very full appendices treat of a number of special subjects.

SOME NEW TESTAMENT PROBLEMS. By ARTHUR WRIGHT, Fellow and Tutor of Queen's College, Cambridge. *Crown 8vo.* 6s.

This book deals with a number of important problems from the standpoint of the 'Higher Criticism,' and is written in the hope of advancing the historico-critical study of the Synoptic Gospels and of the Acts.

The Library of Devotion.

Messrs. METHUEN have arranged to publish under the above title a number of the older masterpieces of devotional literature. It is their intention to entrust each volume of the series to an editor who will not only attempt to bring out the spiritual importance of the book, but who will lavish such scholarly care upon it as is generally expended only on editions of the ancient classics.

The books will be furnished with such Introductions and Notes as may be necessary to explain the standpoint of the author, and to comment on such difficulties as the ordinary reader may find, without unnecessary intrusion between the author and reader.

Mr. Laurence Housman has designed a title-page and a cover design. *Pott 8vo.* 2s.; *leather* 3s.

THE CONFESSIONS OF ST. AUGUSTINE. Newly Translated, with an Introduction and Notes, by C. BIGG, D.D., late Student of Christ Church.

This volume contains the nine books of the 'Confessions' which are suitable for devotional purposes.

THE CHRISTIAN YEAR. By JOHN KEBLE. With Introduction and Notes, by WALTER LOCK, D.D., Warden of Keble College, Ireland Professor at Oxford.

MESSRS. METHUEN'S ANNOUNCEMENTS

THE IMITATION OF CHRIST. A Revised Translation with an Introduction, by C. BIGG, D.D., late Student of Christ Church.

Dr. Bigg has made a practically new translation of this book, which the reader will have, almost for the first time, exactly in the shape in which it left the hands of the author.

A BOOK OF DEVOTIONS. By J. W. STANBRIDGE, M.A., Rector of Bainton, Canon of York, and sometime Fellow of St. John's College, Oxford. *Pott 8vo.*

This book contains devotions, Eucharistic, daily and occasional, for the use of members of the English Church, sufficiently diversified for those who possess other works of the kind. It is intended to be a companion in private and public worship, and is in harmony with the thoughts of the best Devotional writers. ;

General Literature

THE GOLFING PILGRIM. By HORACE G. HUTCHINSON. *Crown 8vo. 6s.*

This book, by a famous golfer, contains the following sketches lightly and humorously written :—The Prologue—The Pilgrim at the Shrine—Mecca out of Season—The Pilgrim at Home—The Pilgrim Abroad—The Life of the Links—A Tragedy by the Way—Scraps from the Scrip—The Golfer in Art—Early Pilgrims in the West —An Interesting Relic.

WORKHOUSES AND PAUPERISM. By LOUISA TWINING. *Crown 8vo. 2s. 6d.* [*Social Questions Series.*

Educational

THE ODES AND EPODES OF HORACE. Translated by A. D. GODLEY, M.A., Fellow of Magdalen College, Oxford. *Crown 8vo. 2s.* [*Classical Translations.*

PASSAGES FOR UNSEEN TRANSLATION. By E. C. MARCHANT, M.A., Fellow of Peterhouse, Cambridge ; and A. M. COOK, M.A., late Scholar of Wadham College, Oxford : Assistant Masters at St. Paul's School. *Crown 8vo. 3s. 6d.*

This book contains Two Hundred Latin and Two Hundred Greek Passages, and has been very carefully compiled to meet the wants of V. and VI. Form Boys at Public Schools. It is also well adapted for the use of Honour men at the Universities.

EASY LATIN EXERCISES ON THE SYNTAX OF THE SHORTER AND REVISED LATIN PRIMER. By A. M. M. STEDMAN, M.A. With Vocabulary. *Seventh and Cheaper Edition. Crown 8vo. 1s. 6d.* Issued with the consent of Dr. Kennedy.

A new and cheaper edition, thoroughly revised by Mr. C. G. Botting, of St. Paul's School.

TEST CARDS IN EUCLID AND ALGEBRA. By D. S. CALDERWOOD, Headmaster of the Normal School, Edinburgh. In a Packet of 40, with Answers. 1s.

A set of cards for advanced pupils in elementary schools.

MESSRS. METHUEN'S ANNOUNCEMENTS 7

Byzantine Texts'
Edited by J. B. BURY, M.A., Professor of Modern History at Trinity College, Dublin.

EVAGRIUS. Edited by PROFESSOR LÉON PARMENTIER of Liége and M. BIDEZ of Gand. *Demy 8vo.*

PSELLUS (HISTORIA). Edited by C. SATHAS. *Demy 8vo.*

Fiction

SIMON DALE. By ANTHONY HOPE. Illustrated by W. ST. J. HARPER. *Crown 8vo. 6s.*
A romance of the reign of Charles II., and Mr. Anthony Hope's first historical novel.

TRAITS AND CONFIDENCES. By The Hon. EMILY LAWLESS, Author of 'Hurrish,' 'Maelcho,' etc. *Crown 8vo. 5s.*

THE VINTAGE. By E. F. BENSON, Author of 'Dodo.' Illustrated by G. P. JACOMB-HOOD. *Crown 8vo. 6s.*
A romance of the Greek War of Independence.

A VOYAGE OF CONSOLATION. By SARA JEANETTE DUNCAN. Author of 'An American Girl in London.' *Crown 8vo. 6s.*
The adventures of an American girl in Europe.

A NEW NOVEL. By B. M. CROKER, Author of 'Proper Pride.' *Crown 8vo. 6s.*

ACROSS THE SALT SEAS. By J. BLOUNDELLE-BURTON. *Crown 8vo. 6s.*

MISS ERIN. By M. E. FRANCIS, Author of 'In a Northern Village.' *Crown 8vo. 6s.*

WILLOWBRAKE. By R. MURRAY GILCHRIST. *Crown 8vo. 6s.*

THE KLOOF BRIDE. By ERNEST GLANVILLE, Author of 'The Fossicker.' Illustrated. *Crown 8vo. 3s. 6d.*
A story of South African Adventure.

BIJLI, THE DANCER. By JAMES BLYTHE PATTON. Illustrated. *Crown 8vo. 6s.*
A Romance of India.

JOSIAH'S WIFE. By NORMA LORIMER. *Crown 8vo. 6s.*

BETWEEN SUN AND SAND. By W. C. SCULLY, Author of 'The White Hecatomb.' *Crown 8vo. 6s.*

CROSS TRAILS. By VICTOR WAITE. Illustrated. *Crown 8vo. 6s.*
A romance of adventure in America and Australia.

THE PHILANTHROPIST. By LUCY MAYNARD. *Crown 8vo. 6s.*

VAUSSORE. By FRANCIS BRUNE. *Crown 8vo. 6s.*

A LIST OF

MESSRS. METHUEN'S PUBLICATIONS

Poetry

RUDYARD KIPLING'S NEW POEMS

Rudyard Kipling. THE SEVEN SEAS. By RUDYARD KIPLING. *Third Edition. Crown 8vo. Buckram, gilt top. 6s.*
'The new poems of Mr. Rudyard Kipling have all the spirit and swing of their predecessors. Patriotism is the solid concrete foundation on which Mr. Kipling has built the whole of his work.'—*Times.*
'The Empire has found a singer; it is no depreciation of the songs to say that statesmen may have, one way or other, to take account of them.'—*Manchester Guardian.*
'Animated through and through with indubitable genius.'—*Daily Telegraph.*
'Packed with inspiration, with humour, with pathos.'—*Daily Chronicle.*
'All the pride of empire, all the intoxication of power, all the ardour, the energy, the masterful strength and the wonderful endurance and death-scorning pluck which are the very bone and fibre and marrow of the British character are here.' —*Daily Mail.*

Rudyard Kipling. BARRACK-ROOM BALLADS. By RUDYARD KIPLING. *Twelfth Edition. Crown 8vo. 6s.*
'Mr. Kipling's verse is strong, vivid, full of character. . . . Unmistakable genius rings in every line.'—*Times.*
'The ballads teem with imagination, they palpitate with emotion. We read them with laughter and tears; the metres throb in our pulses, the cunningly ordered words tingle with life; and if this be not poetry, what is?'—*Pall Mall Gazette.*

'Q.' POEMS AND BALLADS. By "Q." *Crown 8vo. 3s. 6d.*
'This work has just the faint, ineffable touch and glow that make poetry.'—*Speaker.*

"Q." GREEN BAYS: Verses and Parodies. By "Q.," Author of 'Dead Man's Rock,' etc. *Second Edition. Crown 8vo. 3s. 6d.*

E. Mackay. A SONG OF THE SEA. By ERIC MACKAY. *Second Edition. Fcap. 8vo. 5s.*
'Everywhere Mr. Mackay displays himself the master of a style marked by all the characteristics of the best rhetoric.'—*Globe.*

Ibsen. BRAND. A Drama by HENRIK IBSEN. Translated by WILLIAM WILSON. *Second Edition. Crown 8vo. 3s. 6d.*
'The greatest world-poem of the nineteenth century next to "Faust." It is in the same set with "Agamemnon," with "Lear," with the literature that we now instinctively regard as high and holy.'—*Daily Chronicle.*

MESSRS. METHUEN'S LIST 9

"A. G." VERSES TO ORDER. By "A. G." *Cr. 8vo. 2s. 6d. net.*

'A capital specimen of light academic poetry. These verses are very bright and engaging, easy and sufficiently witty.'—*St. James's Gazette.*

Cordery. THE ODYSSEY OF HOMER. A Translation by J. G. CORDERY. *Crown 8vo. 7s. 6d.*

'This new version of the Odyssey fairly deserves a place of honour among its many rivals. Perhaps there is none from which a more accurate knowledge of the original can be gathered with greater pleasure, at least of those that are in metre.'—*Manchester Guardian.*

Belles Lettres, Anthologies, etc.

R. L. Stevenson. VAILIMA LETTERS. By ROBERT LOUIS STEVENSON. With an Etched Portrait by WILLIAM STRANG, and other Illustrations. *Second Edition. Crown 8vo. Buckram. 7s. 6d.*

'Few publications have in our time been more eagerly awaited than these "Vailima Letters," giving the first fruits of the correspondence of Robert Louis Stevenson. But, high as the tide of expectation has run, no reader can possibly be disappointed in the result.'—*St. James's Gazette.*

Henley. ENGLISH LYRICS. Selected and Edited by W. E. HENLEY. *Crown 8vo. Buckram gilt top. 6s.*

'It is a body of choice and lovely poetry.'—*Birmingham Gazette.*
'Mr. Henley's notes, in their brevity and their fulness, their information and their suggestiveness, seem to us a model of what notes should be.'—*Manchester Guardian.*

Henley and Whibley. A BOOK OF ENGLISH PROSE. Collected by W. E. HENLEY and CHARLES WHIBLEY. *Crown 8vo. Buckram gilt top. 6s.*

'A unique volume of extracts—an art gallery of early prose.'—*Birmingham Post.*
'An admirable companion to Mr. Henley's "Lyra Heroica."'—*Saturday Review.*
'Quite delightful. A greater treat for those not well acquainted with pre-Restoration prose could not be imagined.'—*Athenæum.*

H. C. Beeching. LYRA SACRA : An Anthology of Sacred Verse. Edited by H. C. BEECHING, M.A. *Crown 8vo. Buckram. 6s.*

'A charming selection, which maintains a lofty standard of excellence.'—*Times.*

"Q." THE GOLDEN POMP : A Procession of English Lyrics from Surrey to Shirley, arranged by A. T. QUILLER COUCH. *Crown 8vo. Buckram. 6s.*

'A delightful volume : a really golden "Pomp."'—*Spectator.*

W. B. Yeats. AN ANTHOLOGY OF IRISH VERSE. Edited by W. B. YEATS. *Crown 8vo. 3s. 6d.*

'An attractive and catholic selection.'—*Times.*

G. W. Steevens. MONOLOGUES OF THE DEAD. By
G. W. STEEVENS. *Foolscap 8vo.* 3s. 6d.

A series of Soliloquies in which famous men of antiquity—Julius Cæsar, Nero, Alcibiades, etc., attempt to express themselves in the modes of thought and language of to-day.

'The effect is sometimes splendid, sometimes bizarre, but always amazingly clever.'
—*Pall Mall Gazette.*

Victor Hugo. THE LETTERS OF VICTOR HUGO.
Translated from the French by F. CLARKE, M.A. *In Two Volumes.*
Demy 8vo. 10s. 6d. each. *Vol. I.* 1815-35.

C. H. Pearson. ESSAYS AND CRITICAL REVIEWS. By
C. H. PEARSON, M.A., Author of 'National Life and Character.'
With a Portrait. *Demy 8vo.* 10s. 6d.

W. M. Dixon. A PRIMER OF TENNYSON. By W. M.
DIXON, M.A., Professor of English Literature at Mason College.
Crown 8vo. 2s. 6d.

'Much sound and well-expressed criticism and acute literary judgments. The bibliography is a boon.'—*Speaker.*

W. A. Craigie. A PRIMER OF BURNS. By W. A. CRAIGIE.
Crown 8vo. 2s. 6d.

'A valuable addition to the literature of the poet.'—*Times.*
'An admirable introduction.'—*Globe.*

Magnus. A PRIMER OF WORDSWORTH. By LAURIE
MAGNUS. *Crown 8vo.* 2s. 6d.

'A valuable contribution to Wordsworthian literature.'—*Literature.*
'A well-made primer, thoughtful and informing.'—*Manchester Guardian.*

Sterne. THE LIFE AND OPINIONS OF TRISTRAM
SHANDY. By LAWRENCE STERNE. With an Introduction by
CHARLES WHIBLEY, and a Portrait. 2 *vols.* 7s.

'Very dainty volumes are these; the paper, type, and light-green binding are all very agreeable to the eye. *Simplex munditiis* is the phrase that might be applied to them.'—*Globe.*

Congreve. THE COMEDIES OF WILLIAM CONGREVE.
With an Introduction by G. S. STREET, and a Portrait. 2 *vols.* 7s.

Morier. THE ADVENTURES OF HAJJI BABA OF
ISPAHAN. By JAMES MORIER. With an Introduction by E. G.
BROWNE, M.A., and a Portrait. 2 *vols.* 7s.

Walton. THE LIVES OF DONNE, WOTTON, HOOKER,
HERBERT, AND SANDERSON. By IZAAK WALTON. With
an Introduction by VERNON BLACKBURN, and a Portrait. 3s. 6d.

Johnson. THE LIVES OF THE ENGLISH POETS. By
SAMUEL JOHNSON, LL.D. With an Introduction by J. H. MILLAR,
and a Portrait. 3 *vols.* 10s. 6d.

MESSRS. METHUEN'S LIST 11

Burns. THE POEMS OF ROBERT BURNS. Edited by ANDREW LANG and W. A. CRAIGIE. With Portrait. *Demy 8vo, gilt top.* 6s.

This edition contains a carefully collated Text, numerous Notes, critical and textual, a critical and biographical Introduction, and a Glossary.
'Among the editions in one volume, Mr. Andrew Lang's will take the place of authority.'—*Times.*

F. Langbridge. BALLADS OF THE BRAVE : Poems of Chivalry, Enterprise, Courage, and Constancy. Edited by Rev. F. LANGBRIDGE. *Crown 8vo.* 3s. 6d. *School Edition.* 2s. 6d.

'A very happy conception happily carried out. These "Ballads of the Brave" are intended to suit the real tastes of boys, and will suit the taste of the great majority.'—*Spectator.* 'The book is full of splendid things.'—*Word.*

Illustrated Books

Bedford. NURSERY RHYMES. With many Coloured Pictures. By F. D. BEDFORD. *Super Royal 8vo.* 5s.

'An excellent selection of the best known rhymes, with beautifully coloured pictures exquisitely printed.'—*Pall Mall Gazette.*
'The art is of the newest, with well harmonised colouring.'—*Spectator.*

S. Baring Gould. A BOOK OF FAIRY TALES retold by S. BARING GOULD. With numerous illustrations and initial letters by ARTHUR J. GASKIN. *Second Edition. Crown 8vo. Buckram.* 6s.

'Mr. Baring Gould is deserving of gratitude, in re-writing in honest, simple style the old stories that delighted the childhood of "our fathers and grandfathers."'—*Saturday Review.*

S. Baring Gould. OLD ENGLISH FAIRY TALES. Collected and edited by S. BARING GOULD. With Numerous Illustrations by F. D. BEDFORD. *Second Edition. Crown 8vo. Buckram.* 6s.

'A charming volume. The stories have been selected with great ingenuity from various old ballads and folk-tales, and now stand forth, clothed in Mr. Baring Gould's delightful English, to enchant youthful readers.'—*Guardian.*

S. Baring Gould. A BOOK OF NURSERY SONGS AND RHYMES. Edited by S. BARING GOULD, and Illustrated by the Birmingham Art School. *Buckram, gilt top. Crown 8vo.* 6s.

'The volume is very complete in its way, as it contains nursery songs to the number of 77, game-rhymes, and jingles. To the student we commend the sensible introduction, and the explanatory notes.'—*Birmingham Gazette.*

H. C. Beeching. A BOOK OF CHRISTMAS VERSE. Edited by H. C. BEECHING, M.A., and Illustrated by WALTER CRANE. *Crown 8vo, gilt top.* 5s.

A collection of the best verse inspired by the birth of Christ from the Middle Ages to the present day.
An anthology which, from its unity of aim and high poetic excellence, has a better right to exist than most of its fellows.'—*Guardian.*

History

Gibbon. THE DECLINE AND FALL OF THE ROMAN EMPIRE. By EDWARD GIBBON. A New Edition, Edited with Notes, Appendices, and Maps, by J. B. BURY, M.A., Fellow of Trinity College, Dublin. *In Seven Volumes. Demy 8vo. Gilt top. 8s. 6d. each. Also crown 8vo. 6s. each. Vols. I., II., III., and IV.*

'The time has certainly arrived for a new edition of Gibbon's great work. . . . Professor Bury is the right man to undertake this task. His learning is amazing, both in extent and accuracy. The book is issued in a handy form, and at a moderate price, and it is admirably printed.'—*Times.*

'This edition, so far as one may judge from the first instalment, is a marvel of erudition and critical skill, and it is the very minimum of praise to predict that the seven volumes of it will supersede Dean Milman's as the standard edition of our great historical classic.'—*Glasgow Herald.*

'The beau-ideal Gibbon has arrived at last.'—*Sketch.*

'At last there is an adequate modern edition of Gibbon. . . . The best edition the nineteenth century could produce.'—*Manchester Guardian.*

Flinders Petrie. A HISTORY OF EGYPT, FROM THE EARLIEST TIMES TO THE PRESENT DAY. Edited by W. M. FLINDERS PETRIE, D.C.L., LL.D., Professor of Egyptology at University College. *Fully Illustrated. In Six Volumes. Crown 8vo. 6s. each.*

Vol. I. PREHISTORIC TIMES TO XVITH. DYNASTY. W. F. M. Petrie. *Third Edition.*

Vol. II. THE XVIITH AND XVIIITH DYNASTIES. W. M. F. Petrie. *Second Edition.*

'A history written in the spirit of scientific precision so worthily represented by Dr. Petrie and his school cannot but promote sound and accurate study, and supply a vacant place in the English literature of Egyptology.'—*Times.*

Flinders Petrie. EGYPTIAN TALES. Edited by W. M. FLINDERS PETRIE. Illustrated by TRISTRAM ELLIS. *In Two Volumes. Crown 8vo. 3s. 6d. each.*

'A valuable addition to the literature of comparative folk-lore. The drawings are really illustrations in the literal sense of the word.'—*Globe.*

'It has a scientific value to the student of history and archæology.'—*Scotsman.*

'Invaluable as a picture of life in Palestine and Egypt.'—*Daily News.*

Flinders Petrie. EGYPTIAN DECORATIVE ART. By W. M. FLINDERS PETRIE. With 120 Illustrations. *Cr. 8vo. 3s. 6d.*

'Professor Flinders Petrie is not only a profound Egyptologist, but an accomplished student of comparative archæology. In these lectures he displays both qualifications with rare skill in elucidating the development of decorative art in Egypt, and in tracing its influence on the art of other countries.'—*Times.*

S. Baring Gould. THE TRAGEDY OF THE CÆSARS. With numerous Illustrations from Busts, Gems, Cameos, etc. By S. BARING GOULD. *Fourth Edition. Royal 8vo. 15s.*

'A most splendid and fascinating book on a subject of undying interest. The great feature of the book is the use the author has made of the existing portraits of the Caesars, and the admirable critical subtlety he has exhibited in dealing with this line of research. It is brilliantly written, and the illustrations are supplied on a scale of profuse magnificence.'—*Daily Chronicle.*

H. de B. Gibbins. INDUSTRY IN ENGLAND : HISTORICAL OUTLINES. By H. DE B. GIBBINS, M.A., D.Litt. With 5 Maps. *Second Edition. Demy 8vo.* 10s. 6d.
This book is written with the view of affording a clear view of the main facts of English Social and Industrial History placed in due perspective.

H. E. Egerton. A HISTORY OF BRITISH COLONIAL POLICY. By H. E. EGERTON, M.A. *Demy 8vo.* 12s. 6d.
This book deals with British Colonial policy historically from the beginnings of English colonisation down to the present day. The subject has been treated by itself, and it has thus been possible within a reasonable compass to deal with a mass of authority which must otherwise be sought in the State papers. The volume is divided into five parts:—(1) The Period of Beginnings, 1497-1650; (2) Trade Ascendancy, 1651-1830; (3) The Granting of Responsible Government, 1831-1860; (4) *Laissez Aller*, 1861-1885; (5) Greater Britain.
'The whole story of the growth and administration of our colonial empire is comprehensive and well arranged, and is set forth with marked ability.'—*Daily Mail.*
'It is a good book, distinguished by accuracy in detail, clear arrangement of facts, and a broad grasp of principles.'—*Manchester Guardian.*
'Able, impartial, clear. . . . A most valuable volume.'—*Athenæum.*

A. Clark. THE COLLEGES OF OXFORD : Their History and their Traditions. By Members of the University. Edited by A. CLARK, M.A., Fellow and Tutor of Lincoln College. *8vo.* 12s. 6d.
'A work which will certainly be appealed to for many years as the standard book on the Colleges of Oxford.'—*Athenæum.*

Perrens. THE HISTORY OF FLORENCE FROM 1434 TO 1492. By F. T. PERRENS. *8vo.* 12s. 6d.
A history of Florence under the domination of Cosimo, Piero, and Lorenzo de Medicis.

J. Wells. A SHORT HISTORY OF ROME. By J WELLS, M.A., Fellow and Tutor of Wadham Coll., Oxford. With 4 Maps. *Crown 8vo.* 3s. 6d.
This book is intended for the Middle and Upper Forms of Public Schools and for Pass Students at the Universities. It contains copious Tables, etc.
'An original work written on an original plan, and with uncommon freshness and vigour.'—*Speaker.*

O. Browning. A SHORT HISTORY OF MEDIÆVAL ITALY, A.D. 1250-1530. By OSCAR BROWNING, Fellow and Tutor of King's College, Cambridge. *Second Edition. In Two Volumes. Crown 8vo.* 5s. each.
  VOL. I. 1250-1409.—Guelphs and Ghibellines.
  VOL. II. 1409-1530.—The Age of the Condottieri.
'Mr. Browning is to be congratulated on the production of a work of immense labour and learning.'—*Westminster Gazette.*

O'Grady. THE STORY OF IRELAND. By STANDISH O'GRADY, Author of 'Finn and his Companions.' *8vo.* 2s. 6d.
'Most delightful, most stimulating. Its racy humour, its original imaginings, make it one of the freshest, breeziest volumes.'—*Methodist Times.*

Biography

S. Baring Gould. THE LIFE OF NAPOLEON BONAPARTE. By S. BARING GOULD. With over 450 Illustrations in the Text and 12 Photogravure Plates. *Large quarto. Gilt top.* 36s.

'The best biography of Napole in our tongue, nor have the French as good a biographer of their hero. A book very nearly as good as Southey's "Life of Nelson."'—*Manchester Guardian.*

'The main feature of this gorgeous volume is its great wealth of beautiful photogravures and finely-executed wood engravings, constituting a complete pictorial chronicle of Napoleon I.'s personal history from the days of his early childhood at Ajaccio to the date of his second interment under the dome of the Invalides in Paris.'—*Daily Telegraph.*

'Particular notice is due to the vast collection of contemporary illustrations.'—*Guardian.*

'Nearly all the illustrations are real contributions to history.'—*Westminster Gazette.*

Morris Fuller. THE LIFE AND WRITINGS OF JOHN DAVENANT, D.D. (1571-1641), Bishop of Salisbury. By MORRIS FULLER, B.D. *Demy 8vo.* 10s. 6d.

'A valuable contribution to ecclesiastical history.'—*Birmingham Gazette.*

J. M. Rigg. ST. ANSELM OF CANTERBURY: A CHAPTER IN THE HISTORY OF RELIGION. By J. M. RIGG. *Demy 8vo.* 7s. 6d.

'Mr. Rigg has told the story of the great Primate's life with scholarly ability, and has thereby contributed an interesting chapter to the history of the Norman period.'—*Daily Chronicle.*

F. W. Joyce. THE LIFE OF SIR FREDERICK GORE OUSELEY. By F. W. JOYCE, M.A. With Portraits and Illustrations. *Crown 8vo.* 7s. 6d.

'This book has been undertaken in quite the right spirit, and written with sympathy, insight, and considerable literary skill.'—*Times.*

W. G. Collingwood. THE LIFE OF JOHN RUSKIN. By W. G. COLLINGWOOD, M.A. With Portraits, and 13 Drawings by Mr. Ruskin. *Second Edition.* 2 vols. 8vo. 32s.

'No more magnificent volumes have been published for a long time.'—*Times.*
'It is long since we had a biography with such delights of substance and of form. Such a book is a pleasure for the day, and a joy for ever.'—*Daily Chronicle.*

C. Waldstein. JOHN RUSKIN: a Study. By CHARLES WALDSTEIN, M.A., Fellow of King's College, Cambridge. With a Photogravure Portrait after Professor HERKOMER. *Post 8vo.* 5s.

'A thoughtful, impartial, well-written criticism of Ruskin's teaching, intended to separate what the author regards as valuable and permanent from what is transient and erroneous in the great master's writing.'—*Daily Chronicle.*

MESSRS. METHUEN'S LIST 15

Darmesteter. THE LIFE OF ERNEST RENAN. By MADAME DARMESTETER. With Portrait. *Second Edition. Cr. 8vo. 6s.*
A biography of Renan by one of his most intimate friends.
'A polished gem of biography, superior in its kind to any attempt that has been made of recent years in England. Madame Darmesteter has indeed written for English readers "*The* Life of Ernest Renan."'—*Athenæum.*
'It is a fascinating and biographical and critical study, and an admirably finished work of literary art.'—*Scotsman.*
'It is interpenetrated with the dignity and charm, the mild, bright, classical grace of form and treatment that Renan himself so loved ; and it fulfils to the uttermost the delicate and difficult achievement it sets out to accomplish.'—*Academy.*

W. H. Hutton. THE LIFE OF SIR THOMAS MORE. By W. H. HUTTON, M.A. *With Portraits. Crown 8vo. 5s.*
'The book lays good claim to high rank among our biographies. It is excellently, even lovingly, written.'—*Scotsman.*   'An excellent monograph.'—*Times.*

Travel, Adventure and Topography

Johnston. BRITISH CENTRAL AFRICA. By Sir H. H. JOHNSTON, K.C.B. With nearly Two Hundred Illustrations, and Six Maps. *Second Edition. Crown 4to. 30s. net.*
'A fascinating book, written with equal skill and charm—the work at once of a literary artist and of a man of action who is singularly wise, brave, and experienced. It abounds in admirable sketches from pencil.'—*Westminster Gazette.*
'A delightful book . . . collecting within the covers of a single volume all that is known of this part of our African domains. The voluminous appendices are of extreme value.'—*Manchester Guardian.*
'The book takes front rank as a standard work by the one man competent to write it.'—*Daily Chronicle.*
'The book is crowded with important information, and written in a most attractive style ; it is worthy, in short, of the author's established reputation.'—*Standard.*

Prince Henri of Orleans. FROM TONKIN TO INDIA. By PRINCE HENRI OF ORLEANS. Translated by HAMLEY BENT, M.A. With 100 Illustrations and a Map. *Second Edition. Crown 4to, gilt top. 25s.*
The travels of Prince Henri in 1895 from China to the valley of the Bramaputra covered a distance of 2100 miles, of which 1600 was through absolutely unexplored country. No fewer than seventeen ranges of mountains were crossed at altitudes of from 11,000 to 13,000 feet. The journey was made memorable by the discovery of the sources of the Irrawaddy.
'A welcome contribution to our knowledge. The narrative is full and interesting, and the appendices give the work a substantial value.'—*Times.*
'The Prince's travels are of real importance . . . his services to geography have been considerable. The volume is beautifully illustrated.'—*Athenæum.*
'The story is instructive and fascinating, and will certainly make one of the books of 1898. The book attracts by its delightful print and fine illustrations. A nearly model book of travel.'—*Pall Mall Gazette.*
'An entertaining record of pluck and travel in important regions.'—*Daily Chronicle.*
'The illustrations are admirable and quite beyond praise.'—*Glasgow Herald.*
'The Prince's story is charmingly told, and presented with an attractiveness which will make it, in more than one sense, an outstanding book of the season.'—*Birmingham Post.*
'An attractive book which will prove of considerable interest and no little value. A narrative of a remarkable journey.'—*Literature.*
'China is the country of the hour. All eyes are turned towards her, and Messrs. Methuen have opportunely selected the moment to launch Prince Henri's work.'—*Liverpool Daily Post.*

16   MESSRS. METHUENS LIST

R. S. S. Baden-Powell. THE DOWNFALL OF PREMPEH
A Diary of Life in Ashanti, 1895. By Colonel BADEN-POWELL.
With 21 Illustrations and a Map. *Demy 8vo.* 10s. 6d.
'A compact, faithful, most readable record of the campaign.'—*Daily News.*

R. S. S. Baden-Powell. THE MATEBELE CAMPAIGN 1896.
By Colonel BADEN-POWELL. With nearly 100 Illustrations. *Second Edition. Demy 8vo.* 15s.
'As a straightforward account of a great deal of plucky work unpretentiously done, this book is well worth reading. The simplicity of the narrative is all in its favour, and accords in a peculiarly English fashion with the nature of the subject.'—*Times.*

Captain Hinde. THE FALL OF THE CONGO ARABS.
By L. HINDE. With Plans, etc. *Demy 8vo.* 12s. 6d.
'The book is full of good things, and of sustained interest.'—*St. James's Gazette.*
'A graphic sketch of one of the most exciting and important episodes in the struggle for supremacy in Central Africa between the Arabs and their European rivals. Apart from the story of the campaign, Captain Hinde's book is mainly remarkable for the fulness with which he discusses the question of cannibalism. It is, indeed, the only connected narrative—in English, at any rate—which has been published of this particular episode in African history.'—*Times.*

W. Crooke. THE NORTH-WESTERN PROVINCES OF INDIA: THEIR ETHNOLOGY AND ADMINISTRATION. By W. CROOKE. With Maps and Illustrations. *Demy 8vo.* 10s. 6d.
'A carefully and well-written account of one of the most important provinces of the Empire. In seven chapters Mr. Crooke deals successively with the land in its physical aspect, the province under Hindoo and Mussulman rule, the province under British rule, the ethnology and sociology of the province, the religious and social life of the people, the land and its settlement, and the native peasant in his relation to the land. The illustrations are good and well selected, and the map is excellent.'—*Manchester Guardian.*

A. Boisragon. THE BENIN MASSACRE. By CAPTAIN BOISRAGON. With Portrait and Map. *Second Edition. Crown 8vo.* 3s. 6d.
'If the story had been written four hundred years ago it would be read to-day as an English classic.'—*Scotsman.*
'If anything could enhance the horror and the pathos of this remarkable book it is the simple style of the author, who writes as he would talk, unconscious of his own heroism, with an artlessness which is the highest art.'—*Pall Mall Gazette.*

H. S. Cowper. THE HILL OF THE GRACES: OR, THE GREAT STONE TEMPLES OF TRIPOLI. By H. S. COWPER, F.S.A. With Maps, Plans, and 75 Illustrations. *Demy 8vo.* 10s. 6d.
'The book has the interest of all first-hand work, directed by an intelligent man towards a worthy object, and it forms a valuable chapter of what has now become quite a large and important branch of antiquarian research.'—*Times.*

Kinnaird Rose. WITH THE GREEKS IN THESSALY.
By W. KINNAIRD ROSE, Reuter's Correspondent. With Plans and 23 Illustrations. *Crown 8vo.* 6s.

W. B. Worsfold. SOUTH AFRICA. By W. B. WORSFOLD, M.A. *With a Map. Second Edition. Crown 8vo.* 6s.
'A monumental work compressed into a very moderate compass.'—*World.*

Naval and Military

G. W. Steevens. NAVAL POLICY: By. G. W. STEEVENS. *Demy 8vo. 6s.*

This book is a description of the British and other more important navies of the world, with a sketch of the lines on which our naval policy might possibly be developed.
'An extremely able and interesting work.'—*Daily Chronicle.*

D. Hannay. A SHORT HISTORY OF THE ROYAL NAVY, FROM EARLY TIMES TO THE PRESENT DAY. By DAVID HANNAY. Illustrated. 2 Vols. *Demy 8vo. 7s. 6d. each.* Vol. I., 1200-1688.

'We read it from cover to cover at a sitting, and those who go to it for a lively and brisk picture of the past, with all its faults and its grandeur, will not be disappointed. The historian is competent, and he is endowed with literary skill and style.'— *Standard.*
'We can warmly recommend Mr. Hannay's volume to any intelligent student of naval history. Great as is the merit of Mr. Hannay's historical narrative, the merit of his strategic exposition is even greater.'—*Times.*
'His book is brisk and pleasant reading, for he is gifted with a most agreeable style. His reflections are philosophical, and he has seized and emphasised just those points which are of interest.'—*Graphic.*

Cooper King. THE STORY OF THE BRITISH ARMY. By Lieut.-Colonel COOPER KING, of the Staff College, Camberley. Illustrated. *Demy 8vo. 7s. 6d.*

'An authoritative and accurate story of England's military progress.'—*Daily Mail.*
'This handy volume contains, in a compendious form, a brief but adequate sketch of the story of the British army.'—*Daily News.*

R. Southey. ENGLISH SEAMEN (Howard, Clifford, Hawkins, Drake, Cavendish). By ROBERT SOUTHEY. Edited, with an Introduction, by DAVID HANNAY. *Second Edition. Crown 8vo. 6s.*

'Admirable and well-told stories of our naval history.'—*Army and Navy Gazette.*
'A brave, inspiriting book.'—*Black and White.*

W. Clark Russell. THE LIFE OF ADMIRAL LORD COLLINGWOOD. By W. CLARK RUSSELL, With Illustrations by F. BRANGWYN. *Third Edition. Crown 8vo. 6s.*

'A book which we should like to see in the hands of every boy in the country.'—*St. James's Gazette.* 'A really good book.'—*Saturday Review.*

E. L. S. Horsburgh. THE CAMPAIGN OF WATERLOO. By E. L. S. HORSBURGH, B.A. *With Plans. Crown 8vo. 5s.*

'A brilliant essay—simple, sound, and thorough.'—*Daily Chronicle.*

H. B. George. BATTLES OF ENGLISH HISTORY. By H. B. GEORGE, M.A., Fellow of New College, Oxford. *With numerous Plans. Third Edition. Crown 8vo. 6s.*

'Mr. George has undertaken a very useful task—that of making military affairs intelligible and instructive to non-military readers—and has executed it with laudable intelligence and industry, and with a large measure of success.'—*Times.*

General Literature

S. Baring Gould. OLD COUNTRY LIFE. By S. BARING GOULD. With Sixty-seven Illustrations. *Large Crown 8vo. Fifth Edition.* 6s.

'"Old Country Life," as healthy wholesome reading, full of breezy life and movement, full of quaint stories vigorously told, will not be excelled by any book to be published throughout the year. Sound, hearty, and English to the core.'—*World.*

S. Baring Gould. HISTORIC ODDITIES AND STRANGE EVENTS. By S. BARING GOULD. *Fourth Edition. Crown 8vo.* 6s.

'A collection of exciting and entertaining chapters. The whole volume is delightful reading.'—*Times.*

S. Baring Gould. FREAKS OF FANATICISM. By S. BARING GOULD. *Third Edition. Crown 8vo.* 6s.

'Mr. Baring Gould has a keen eye for colour and effect, and the subjects he has chosen give ample scope to his descriptive and analytic faculties. A perfectly fascinating book.'—*Scottish Leader.*

S. Baring Gould. A GARLAND OF COUNTRY SONG: English Folk Songs with their Traditional Melodies. Collected and arranged by S. BARING GOULD and H. F. SHEPPARD. *Demy 4to.* 6s.

S. Baring Gould. SONGS OF THE WEST: Traditional Ballads and Songs of the West of England, with their Traditional Melodies. Collected by S. BARING GOULD, M.A., and H. F. SHEPPARD, M.A. Arranged for Voice and Piano. In 4 Parts. Parts I., II., III., 3s. each. Part IV., 5s. *In one Vol., French morocco,* 15s.

'A rich collection of humour, pathos, grace, and poetic fancy.'—*Saturday Review.*

S. Baring Gould. YORKSHIRE ODDITIES AND STRANGE EVENTS. *Fourth Edition. Crown 8vo.* 6s.

S. Baring Gould. STRANGE SURVIVALS AND SUPERSTITIONS. With Illustrations. By S. BARING GOULD. *Crown 8vo. Second Edition.* 6s.

S. Baring Gould. THE DESERTS OF SOUTHERN FRANCE. By S. BARING GOULD. 2 vols. *Demy 8vo.* 32s.

Cotton Minchin. OLD HARROW DAYS. By J. G. COTTON MINCHIN. *Crown 8vo. Second Edition.* 5s.

'This book is an admirable record.'—*Daily Chronicle.*
'Mr. Cotton Minchin's bright and breezy reminiscences of 'Old Harrow Days' will delight all Harrovians, old and young, and may go far to explain the abiding enthusiasm of old Harrovians for their school to readers who have not been privileged to be their schoolfellows.'—*Times.*

W. E. Gladstone. THE SPEECHES OF THE RT. HON. W. E. GLADSTONE, M.P. Edited by A. W. HUTTON, M.A., and H. J. COHEN, M.A. With Portraits. *8vo. Vols. IX. and X.* 12s. 6d. each.

J. Wells. OXFORD AND OXFORD LIFE. By Members of the University. Edited by J. WELLS, M.A., Fellow and Tutor of Wadham College. *Crown 8vo. 3s. 6d.*
'We congratulate Mr. Wells on the production of a readable and intelligent account of Oxford as it is at the present time, written by persons who are possessed of a close acquaintance with the system and life of the University.'—*Athenæum.*

J. Wells. OXFORD AND ITS COLLEGES. By J. WELLS, M.A., Fellow and Tutor of Wadham College. Illustrated by E. H. NEW. *Second Edition. Fcap. 8vo. 3s. Leather. 4s.*
This is a guide—chiefly historical—to the Colleges of Oxford. It contains numerous illustrations.
'An admirable and accurate little treatise, attractively illustrated.'—*World.*
'A luminous and tasteful little volume.'—*Daily Chronicle.*
'Exactly what the intelligent visitor wants.'—*Glasgow Herald.*

C. G. Robertson. VOCES ACADEMICÆ. By C. GRANT ROBERTSON, M.A., Fellow of All Souls', Oxford. *With a Frontispiece. Pott. 8vo. 3s. 6d.*
'Decidedly clever and amusing.'—*Athenæum.*
'The dialogues are abundantly smart and amusing.'—*Glasgow Herald.*
'A clever and entertaining little book.'—*Pall Mall Gazette.*

L. Whibley. GREEK OLIGARCHIES : THEIR ORGANISATION AND CHARACTER. By L. WHIBLEY, M.A., Fellow of Pembroke College, Cambridge. *Crown 8vo. 6s.*
'An exceedingly useful handbook: a careful and well-arranged study.'—*Times.*

L. L. Price. ECONOMIC SCIENCE AND PRACTICE. By L. L. PRICE, M.A., Fellow of Oriel College, Oxford. *Crown 8vo. 6s.*
'The book is well written, giving evidence of considerable literary ability, and clear mental grasp of the subject under consideration.'—*Western Morning News.*

J. S. Shedlock. THE PIANOFORTE SONATA : Its Origin and Development. By J. S. SHEDLOCK. *Crown 8vo. 5s.*
'This work should be in the possession of every musician and amateur. A concise and lucid history of the origin of one of the most important forms of musical composition. A very valuable work for reference.'—*Athenæum.*

E. M. Bowden. THE EXAMPLE OF BUDDHA: Being Quotations from Buddhist Literature for each Day in the Year. Compiled by E. M. BOWDEN. *Third Edition. 16mo. 2s. 6d.*

Morgan-Browne. SPORTING AND ATHLETIC RECORDS. By H. MORGAN-BROWNE. *Crown 8vo.* 1s. *paper*; 1s. 6d. *cloth.*
'Should meet a very wide demand.'—*Daily Mail.*
'A very careful collection, and the first one of its kind.'—*Manchester Guardian.*
'Certainly the most valuable of all books of its kind.'—*Birmingham Gazette.*

Science

Freudenreich. DAIRY BACTERIOLOGY. A Short Manual for the Use of Students. By Dr. ED. VON FREUDENREICH. Translated by J. R. AINSWORTH DAVIS, B.A. *Crown 8vo. 2s. 6d.*

Chalmers Mitchell. OUTLINES OF BIOLOGY. By P. CHALMERS MITCHELL, M.A., *Illustrated.* *Crown 8vo.* 6s.

A text-book designed to cover the new Schedule issued by the Royal College of Physicians and Surgeons.

G. Massee. A MONOGRAPH OF THE MYXOGASTRES. By GEORGE MASSEE. With 12 Coloured Plates. *Royal 8vo.* 18s. *net.*

'A work much in advance of any book in the language treating of this group of organisms. Indispensable to every student of the Myxogastres.'—*Nature.*

Technology

Stephenson and Suddards. ORNAMENTAL DESIGN FOR WOVEN FABRICS. By C. STEPHENSON, of The Technical College, Bradford, and F. SUDDARDS, of The Yorkshire College, Leeds. With 65 full-page plates, and numerous designs and diagrams in the text. *Demy 8vo.* 7s. 6d.

'The book is very ably done, displaying an intimate knowledge of principles, good taste, and the faculty of clear exposition.'—*Yorkshire Post.*

HANDBOOKS OF TECHNOLOGY.
Edited by PROFESSORS GARNETT and WERTHEIMER.

HOW TO MAKE A DRESS. By J. A. E. WOOD. *Illustrated.* *Crown 8vo.* 1s. 6d.

A text-book for students preparing for the City and Guilds examination, based on the syllabus. The diagrams are numerous.

'Though primarily intended for students, Miss Wood's dainty little manual may be consulted with advantage by any girls who want to make their own frocks. The directions are simple and clear, and the diagrams very helpful.'—*Literature.*
'A splendid little book.'—*Evening News.*

Philosophy

L. T. Hobhouse. THE THEORY OF KNOWLEDGE. By L. T. HOBHOUSE, Fellow of C.C.C, Oxford. *Demy 8vo.* 21s.

'The most important contribution to English philosophy since the publication of Mr. Bradley's "Appearance and Reality." Full of brilliant criticism and of positive theories which are models of lucid statement.'—*Glasgow Herald.*
'A brilliantly written volume.'—*Times.*

W. H. Fairbrother. THE PHILOSOPHY OF T. H. GREEN. By W. H. FAIRBROTHER, M.A. *Crown 8vo.* 3s. 6d.

'In every way an admirable book.'—*Glasgow Herald.*

F. W. Bussell. THE SCHOOL OF PLATO : its Origin and its Revival under the Roman Empire. By F. W. BUSSELL, D.D., Fellow and Tutor of Brasenose College, Oxford. *Demy 8vo.* 10s. 6d.

'A highly valuable contribution to the history of ancient thought.'—*Glasgow Herald.*
'A clever and stimulating book, provocative of thought and deserving careful reading.'—*Manchester Guardian.*

F. S. Granger. THE WORSHIP OF THE ROMANS. By F. S. GRANGER, M.A., Litt.D., Professor of Philosophy at University College, Nottingham. *Crown 8vo.* 6s.

'A scholarly analysis of the religious ceremonies, beliefs, and superstitions of ancient Rome, conducted in the new light of comparative anthropology.'—*Times.*

Theology

HANDBOOKS OF THEOLOGY.

General Editor, A. ROBERTSON, D.D., Principal of King's College, London.

THE XXXIX. ARTICLES OF THE CHURCH OF ENGLAND. Edited with an Introduction by E. C. S. GIBSON, D.D., Vicar of Leeds, late Principal of Wells Theological College. *Second and Cheaper Edition in One Volume. Demy 8vo.* 12s. 6d.

'Dr. Gibson is a master of clear and orderly exposition, and he has enlisted in his service all the mechanism of variety of type which so greatly helps to elucidate a complicated subject. And he has in a high degree a quality very necessary, but rarely found, in commentators on this topic, that of absolute fairness. His book is pre-eminently honest.'—*Times.*

'After a survey of the whole book, we can bear witness to the transparent honesty of purpose, evident industry, and clearness of style which mark its contents. They maintain throughout a very high level of doctrine and tone.'—*Guardian.*

'An elaborate and learned book, excellently adapted to its purpose.'—*Speaker.*

'The most convenient and most acceptable commentary.'—*Expository Times.*

AN INTRODUCTION TO THE HISTORY OF RELIGION. By F. B. JEVONS, M.A., Litt.D., Principal of Bishop Hatfield's Hall. *Demy 8vo.* 10s. 6d.

'Dr. Jevons has written a notable work, which we can strongly recommend to the serious attention of theologians and anthropologists.'—*Manchester Guardian.*

'The merit of this book lies in the penetration, the singular acuteness and force of the author's judgment. He is at once critical and luminous, at once just and suggestive. A comprehensive and thorough book.'—*Birmingham Post.*

THE DOCTRINE OF THE INCARNATION. By R. L. OTTLEY, M.A., late fellow of Magdalen College, Oxon., and Principal of Pusey House. *In Two Volumes. Demy 8vo.* 15s.

'Learned and reverent: lucid and well arranged.'—*Record.*

'Accurate, well ordered, and judicious.'—*National Observer.*

'A clear and remarkably full account of the main currents of speculation. Scholarly precision . . . genuine tolerance . . . intense interest in his subject—are Mr. Ottley's merits.'—*Guardian.*

C. F. Andrews. CHRISTIANITY AND THE LABOUR QUESTION. By C. F. ANDREWS, B.A. *Crown 8vo.* 2s. 6d.

S. R. Driver. SERMONS ON SUBJECTS CONNECTED WITH THE OLD TESTAMENT. By S. R. DRIVER, D.D., Canon of Christ Church, Regius Professor of Hebrew in the University of Oxford. *Crown 8vo.* 6s.

'A welcome companion to the author's famous 'Introduction.' No man can read these discourses without feeling that Dr. Driver is fully alive to the deeper teaching of the Old Testament.'—*Guardian.*

T. K. Cheyne. FOUNDERS OF OLD TESTAMENT CRITICISM. By T. K. CHEYNE, D.D., Oriel Professor at Oxford. *Large crown 8vo. 7s. 6d.*

This book is a historical sketch of O. T. Criticism in the form of biographical studies from the days of Eichhorn to those of Driver and Robertson Smith.
'A very learned and instructive work.'—*Times.*

H. H. Henson. LIGHT AND LEAVEN : HISTORICAL AND SOCIAL SERMONS. By the Rev. H. HENSLEY HENSON, M.A., Fellow of All Souls', Incumbent of St. Mary's Hospital, Ilford. *Crown 8vo. 6s.*

'They are always reasonable as well as vigorous, and they are none the less impressive because they regard the needs of a life on this side of a hereafter.'—*Scotsman.*

W. H. Bennett. A PRIMER OF THE BIBLE. By Prof. W. H. BENNETT. *Second Edition. Crown 8vo. 2s. 6d.*

'The work of an honest, fearless, and sound critic, and an excellent guide in a small compass to the books of the Bible.'—*Manchester Guardian,*
'A unique primer. Mr. Bennett has collected and condensed a very extensive and diversified amount of material, and no one can consult his pages and fail to acknowledge indebtedness to his undertaking.'—*English Churchman.*

C. H. Prior. CAMBRIDGE SERMONS. Edited by C. H. PRIOR, M.A., Fellow and Tutor of Pembroke College. *Crown 8vo. 6s.*

A volume of sermons preached before the University of Cambridge by various preachers, including the late Archbishop of Canterbury and Bishop Westcott.

E. B. Layard. RELIGION IN BOYHOOD. Notes on the Religious Training of Boys. By E. B. LAYARD, M.A. *18mo. 1s.*

W. Yorke Faussett. THE *DE CATECHIZANDIS RUDIBUS* OF ST. AUGUSTINE. Edited, with Introduction, Notes, etc., by W. YORKE FAUSSETT, M.A., late Scholar of Balliol Coll. *Crown 8vo. 3s. 6d.*

An edition of a Treatise on the Essentials of Christian Doctrine, and the best methods of impressing them on candidates for baptism.

A Kempis. THE IMITATION OF CHRIST. By THOMAS À KEMPIS. With an Introduction by DEAN FARRAR. Illustrated by C. M. GERE, and printed in black and red. *Second Edition. Fcap. 8vo. Buckram. 3s. 6d. Padded morocco, 5s.*

'Amongst all the innumerable English editions of the "Imitation," there can have been few which were prettier than this one, printed in strong and handsome type, with all the glory of red initials.'—*Glasgow Herald.*

J. Keble. THE CHRISTIAN YEAR. By JOHN KEBLE. With an Introduction and Notes by W. LOCK, D.D., Warden of Keble College, Ireland Professor at Oxford. Illustrated by R. ANNING BELL. *Second Edition. Fcap. 8vo. Buckram. 3s. 6d. Padded morocco, 5s.*

'The present edition is annotated with all the care and insight to be expected from Mr. Lock. The progress and circumstances of its composition are detailed in the Introduction. There is an interesting Appendix on the MSS. of the "Christian Year," and another giving the order in which the poems were written. A "Short Analysis of the Thought" is prefixed to each, and any difficulty in the text is explained in a note.'—*Guardian.*

Leaders of Religion

Edited by H. C. BEECHING, M.A. *With Portraits, crown 8vo.*

A series of short biographies of the most prominent leaders of religious life and thought of all ages and countries.

The following are ready—

CARDINAL NEWMAN. By R. H. HUTTON.
JOHN WESLEY. By J. H. OVERTON, M.A.
BISHOP WILBERFORCE. By G. W. DANIEL, M.A.
CARDINAL MANNING. By A. W. HUTTON, M.A.
CHARLES SIMEON. By H. C. G. MOULE, M.A.
JOHN KEBLE. By WALTER LOCK, D.D.
THOMAS CHALMERS. By Mrs. OLIPHANT.
LANCELOT ANDREWES. By R. L. OTTLEY, M.A.
AUGUSTINE OF CANTERBURY. By E. L. CUTTS, D.D.
WILLIAM LAUD. By W. H. HUTTON, B.D.
JOHN KNOX. By F. M'CUNN.
JOHN HOWE. By R. F. HORTON, D.D.
BISHOP KEN. By F. A. CLARKE, M.A.
GEORGE FOX, THE QUAKER. By T. HODGKIN, D.C.L.
JOHN DONNE. By AUGUSTUS JESSOPP, D.D.

Other volumes will be announced in due course.

Fiction

SIX SHILLING NOVELS

Marie Corelli's Novels

Crown 8vo. 6s. each.

A ROMANCE OF TWO WORLDS. *Seventeenth Edition.*
VENDETTA. *Thirteenth Edition.*
THELMA. *Seventeenth Edition.*
ARDATH. *Eleventh Edition.*
THE SOUL OF LILITH. *Ninth Edition.*
WORMWOOD. *Eighth Edition.*
BARABBAS: A DREAM OF THE WORLD'S TRAGEDY. *Thirty-first Edition.*

'The tender reverence of the treatment and the imaginative beauty of the writing have reconciled us to the daring of the conception, and the conviction is forced on us that even so exalted a subject cannot be made too familiar to us, provided it be presented in the true spirit of Christian faith. The amplifications of the Scripture narrative are often conceived with high poetic insight, and this "Dream of the World's Tragedy" is, despite some trifling incongruities, a lofty and not inadequate paraphrase of the supreme climax of the inspired narrative.'—*Dublin Review.*

MESSRS. METHUEN'S LIST

THE SORROWS OF SATAN. *Thirty-sixth Edition.*

'A very powerful piece of work. . . . The conception is magnificent, and is likely to win an abiding place within the memory of man. . . . The author has immense command of language, and a limitless audacity. . . . This interesting and remarkable romance will live long after much of the ephemeral literature of the day is forgotten. . . . A literary phenomenon . . . novel, and even sublime.'—W. T. STEAD in the *Review of Reviews.*

Anthony Hope's Novels
Crown 8vo. 6s. each.

THE GOD IN THE CAR. *Seventh Edition.*

'A very remarkable book, deserving of critical analysis impossible within our limit; brilliant, but not superficial; well considered, but not elaborated; constructed with the proverbial art that conceals, but yet allows itself to be enjoyed by readers to whom fine literary method is a keen pleasure.'—*The World.*

A CHANGE OF AIR. *Fourth Edition.*

'A graceful, vivacious comedy, true to human nature. The characters are traced with a masterly hand.'—*Times.*

A MAN OF MARK. *Fourth Edition.*

'Of all Mr. Hope's books, "A Man of Mark" is the one which best compares with "The Prisoner of Zenda."'—*National Observer.*

THE CHRONICLES OF COUNT ANTONIO. *Third Edition.*

'It is a perfectly enchanting story of love and chivalry, and pure romance. The Count is the most constant, desperate, and modest and tender of lovers, a peerless gentleman, an intrepid fighter, a faithful friend, and a magnanimous foe.'—*Guardian.*

PHROSO. Illustrated by H. R. MILLAR. *Third Edition.*

'The tale is thoroughly fresh, quick with vitality, stirring the blood, and humorously, dashingly told.'—*St. James's Gazette.*
'A story of adventure, every page of which is palpitating with action.'—*Speaker.*
'From cover to cover "Phroso" not only engages the attention, but carries the reader in little whirls of delight from adventure to adventure.'—*Academy.*

S. Baring Gould's Novels
Crown 8vo. 6s. each.

'To say that a book is by the author of "Mehalah" is to imply that it contains a story cast on strong lines, containing dramatic possibilities, vivid and sympathetic descriptions of Nature, and a wealth of ingenious imagery.'—*Speaker.*
'That whatever Mr. Baring Gould writes is well worth reading, is a conclusion that may be very generally accepted. His views of life are fresh and vigorous, his language pointed and characteristic, the incidents of which he makes use are striking and original, his characters are life-like, and though somewhat exceptional people, are drawn and coloured with artistic force. Add to this that his descriptions of scenes and scenery are painted with the loving eyes and skilled hands of a master of his art, that he is always fresh and never dull, and under such conditions it is no wonder that readers have gained confidence both in his power of amusing and satisfying them, and that year by year his popularity widens.'—*Court Circular.*

ARMINELL : A Social Romance. *Fourth Edition.*

URITH : A Story of Dartmoor. *Fifth Edition.*

'The author is at his best.'—*Times.*

IN THE ROAR OF THE SEA. *Sixth Edition.*
'One of the best imagined and most enthralling stories the author has produced.'
—*Saturday Review.*

MRS. CURGENVEN OF CURGENVEN. *Fourth Edition.*
'The swing of the narrative is splendid.'—*Sussex Daily News.*

CHEAP JACK ZITA. *Fourth Edition.*
'A powerful drama of human passion.'—*Westminster Gazette.*
'A story worthy the author.'—*National Observer.*

THE QUEEN OF LOVE. *Fourth Edition.*
'Can be heartily recommended to all who care for cleanly, energetic, and interesting fiction.'—*Sussex Daily News.*

KITTY ALONE. *Fourth Edition.*
'A strong and original story, teeming with graphic description, stirring incident, and, above all, with vivid and enthralling human interest.'—*Daily Telegraph.*

NOÉMI: A Romance of the Cave-Dwellers. Illustrated by R. CATON WOODVILLE. *Third Edition.*
'A powerful story, full of strong lights and shadows.'—*Standard.*

THE BROOM-SQUIRE. Illustrated by FRANK DADD. *Fourth Edition.*
'A strain of tenderness is woven through the web of his tragic tale, and its atmosphere is sweetened by the nobility and sweetness of the heroine's character.'—*Daily News.*

THE PENNYCOMEQUICKS. *Third Edition.*

DARTMOOR IDYLLS.
'A book to read, and keep and read again; for the genuine fun and pathos of it will not early lose their effect.'—*Vanity Fair.*

GUAVAS THE TINNER. Illustrated by FRANK DADD. *Second Edition.*
'There is a kind of flavour about this book which alone elevates it above the ordinary novel. The story itself has a grandeur in harmony with the wild and rugged scenery which is its setting.'—*Athenæum.*

BLADYS. *Second Edition.*
'A story of thrilling interest.'—*Scotsman.*
'A sombre but powerful story.'—*Daily Mail.*

Gilbert Parker's Novels

Crown 8vo. 6s. each.

PIERRE AND HIS PEOPLE. *Fourth Edition.*
'Stories happily conceived and finely executed. There is strength and genius in Mr. Parker's style.'—*Daily Telegraph.*

MRS. FALCHION. *Fourth Edition.*
'A splendid study of character.'—*Athenæum.*
'But little behind anything that has been done by any writer of our time.'—*Pall Mall Gazette.* 'A very striking and admirable novel.'—*St. James's Gazette.*

THE TRANSLATION OF A SAVAGE.
'The plot is original and one difficult to work out; but Mr. Parker has done it with great skill and delicacy. The reader who is not interested in this original, fresh, and well-told tale must be a dull person indeed.'—*Daily Chronicle.*

MESSRS. METHUEN'S LIST

THE TRAIL OF THE SWORD. *Fifth Edition.*
'A rousing and dramatic tale. A book like this, in which swords flash, great surprises are undertaken, and daring deeds done, in which men and women live and love in the old passionate way, is a joy inexpressible.'—*Daily Chronicle.*

WHEN VALMOND CAME TO PONTIAC: The Story of a Lost Napoleon. *Fourth Edition.*
'Here we find romance—real, breathing, living romance. The character of Valmond is drawn unerringly. The book must be read, we may say re-read, for any one thoroughly to appreciate Mr. Parker's delicate touch and innate sympathy with humanity.'—*Pall Mall Gazette.*

AN ADVENTURER OF THE NORTH: The Last Adventures of 'Pretty Pierre.' *Second Edition.*
'The present book is full of fine and moving stories of the great North, and it will add to Mr. Parker's already high reputation.'—*Glasgow Herald.*

THE SEATS OF THE MIGHTY. *Illustrated. Ninth Edition.*
'The best thing he has done; one of the best things that any one has done lately.'—*St. James's Gazette.*
'Mr. Parker seems to become stronger and easier with every serious novel that he attempts. He shows the matured power which his former novels have led us to expect, and has produced a really fine historical novel. The finest novel he has yet written.'—*Athenæum.*
'A great book.'—*Black and White.*
'One of the strongest stories of historical interest and adventure that we have read for many a day. . . . A notable and successful book.'—*Speaker.*

THE POMP OF THE LAVILETTES. *Second Edition.* 3s. 6d.
'Living, breathing romance, genuine and unforced pathos, and a deeper and more subtle knowledge of human nature than Mr. Parker has ever displayed before. It is, in a word, the work of a true artist.'—*Pall Mall Gazette.*

Conan Doyle. ROUND THE RED LAMP. By A. CONAN DOYLE, Author of 'The White Company,' 'The Adventures of Sherlock Holmes,' etc. *Fifth Edition. Crown 8vo. 6s.*
'The book is, indeed, composed of leaves from life, and is far and away the best view that has been vouchsafed us behind the scenes of the consulting-room. It is very superior to "The Diary of a late Physician."'—*Illustrated London News.*

Stanley Weyman. UNDER THE RED ROBE. By STANLEY WEYMAN, Author of 'A Gentleman of France.' With Twelve Illustrations by R. Caton Woodville. *Twelfth Edition. Crown 8vo. 6s.*
'A book of which we have read every word for the sheer pleasure of reading, and which we put down with a pang that we cannot forget it all and start again.'—*Westminster Gazette.*
'Every one who reads books at all must read this thrilling romance, from the first page of which to the last the breathless reader is haled along. An inspiration of manliness and courage.'—*Daily Chronicle.*

Lucas Malet. THE WAGES OF SIN. By LUCAS MALET. *Thirteenth Edition. Crown 8vo. 6s.*

Lucas Malet. THE CARISSIMA. By LUCAS MALET, Author of 'The Wages of Sin,' etc. *Third Edition. Crown 8vo. 6s.*

S. R. Crockett. LOCHINVAR. By S. R. CROCKETT, Author of 'The Raiders,' etc. Illustrated. *Second Edition. Crown 8vo.* 6s.

'Full of gallantry and pathos, of the clash of arms, and brightened by episodes of humour and love. . . . Mr. Crockett has never written a stronger or better book. An engrossing and fascinating story. The love story alone is enough to make the book delightful.'—*Westminster Gazette.*

Arthur Morrison. TALES OF MEAN STREETS. By ARTHUR MORRISON. *Fourth Edition. Crown 8vo.* 6s.

'Told with consummate art and extraordinary detail. In the true humanity of the book lies its justification, the permanence of its interest, and its indubitable triumph.'—*Athenæum.*
'A great book. The author's method is amazingly effective, and produces a thrilling sense of reality. The writer lays upon us a master hand. The book is simply appalling and irresistible in its interest. It is humorous also ; without humour it would not make the mark it is certain to make.'—*World.*

Arthur Morrison. A CHILD OF THE JAGO. By ARTHUR MORRISON. *Third Edition. Crown 8vo.* 6s.

'The book is a masterpiece.'—*Pall Mall Gazette.*
'Told with great vigour and powerful simplicity.'—*Athenæum.*

Mrs. Clifford. A FLASH OF SUMMER. By Mrs. W. K. CLIFFORD, Author of 'Aunt Anne,' etc. *Second Edition. Crown 8vo.* 6s.

'The story is a very sad and a very beautiful one, exquisitely told, and enriched with many subtle touches of wise and tender insight.'—*Speaker.*

Emily Lawless. HURRISH. By the Honble. EMILY LAWLESS, Author of 'Maelcho,' etc. *Fifth Edition. Crown 8vo.* 6s.

A reissue of Miss Lawless' most popular novel, uniform with 'Maelcho.'

Emily Lawless. MAELCHO : a Sixteenth Century Romance. By the Honble. EMILY LAWLESS. *Second Edition. Crown 8vo.* 6s.

'A really great book.'—*Spectator.*
'There is no keener pleasure in life than the recognition of genius. A piece of work of the first order, which we do not hesitate to describe as one of the most remarkable literary achievements of this generation.'—*Manchester Guardian.*

Jane Barlow. A CREEL OF IRISH STORIES. By JANE BARLOW, Author of 'Irish Idylls.' *Second Edition. Crown 8vo.* 6s.

'Vivid and singularly real.'—*Scotsman.*
'Genuinely and naturally Irish.'—*Scotsman.*
'The sincerity of her sentiments, the distinction of her style, and the freshness of her themes, combine to lift her work far above the average level of contemporary fiction.'—*Manchester Guardian.*

J. H. Findlater. THE GREEN GRAVES OF BALGOWRIE. By JANE H. FINDLATER. *Fourth Edition. Crown 8vo.* 6s.

'A powerful and vivid story.'—*Standard.*
'A beautiful story, sad and strange as truth itself.'—*Vanity Fair.*
'A work of remarkable interest and originality.'—*National Observer.*
'A very charming and pathetic tale.'—*Pall Mall Gazette.*
'A singularly original, clever, and beautiful story.'—*Guardian.*
'Reveals to us a new writer of undoubted faculty and reserve force.'—*Spectator.*
'An exquisite idyll, delicate, affecting, and beautiful.'—*Black and White.*

J. H. Findlater. A DAUGHTER OF STRIFE. By JANE HELEN FINDLATER, Author of 'The Green Graves of Balgowrie.' *Crown 8vo.* 6s.

'A story of strong human interest.'—*Scotsman.*
'It has a sweet flavour of olden days delicately conveyed.'—*Manchester Guardian.*
'Her thought has solidity and maturity.'—*Daily Mail.*

Mary Findlater. OVER THE HILLS. By MARY FINDLATER. *Crown 8vo.* 6s.

'A strong and fascinating piece of work.'—*Scotsman.*
'A charming romance, and full of incident. The book is fresh and strong.'—*Speaker.*
'There is quiet force and beautiful simplicity in this book which will make the author's name loved in many a household.'—*Literary World.*
'Admirably fresh and broad in treatment. The novel is markedly original and excellently written.'—*Daily Chronicle.*
'A strong and wise book of deep insight and unflinching truth.'—*Birmingham Post.*
'Miss Mary Findlater combines originality with strength.'—*Daily Mail.*

H. G. Wells. THE STOLEN BACILLUS, and other Stories. By H. G. WELLS. *Second Edition. Crown 8vo.* 6s.

'The ordinary reader of fiction may be glad to know that these stories are eminently readable from one cover to the other, but they are more than that; they are the impressions of a very striking imagination, which, it would seem, has a great deal within its reach.'—*Saturday Review.*

H. G. Wells. THE PLATTNER STORY AND OTHERS. By H. G. WELLS. *Second Edition. Crown 8vo.* 6s.

'Weird and mysterious, they seem to hold the reader as by a magic spell.'—*Scotsman.*
'No volume has appeared for a long time so likely to give equal pleasure to the simplest reader and to the most fastidious critic.'—*Academy.*

E. F. Benson. DODO: A DETAIL OF THE DAY. By E. F. BENSON. *Sixteenth Edition. Crown 8vo.* 6s.

'A delightfully witty sketch of society.'—*Spectator.*
'A perpetual feast of epigram and paradox.'—*Speaker.*

E. F. Benson. THE RUBICON. By E. F. BENSON, Author of 'Dodo.' *Fifth Edition. Crown 8vo.* 6s.

Mrs. Oliphant. SIR ROBERT'S FORTUNE. By MRS. OLIPHANT. *Crown 8vo.* 6s.

'Full of her own peculiar charm of style and simple, subtle character-painting comes her new gift, the delightful story.'—*Pall Mall Gazette.*

Mrs. Oliphant. THE TWO MARYS. By MRS. OLIPHANT. *Second Edition. Crown 8vo.* 6s.

Mrs. Oliphant. THE LADY'S WALK. By Mrs. OLIPHANT. *Second Edition. Crown 8vo.* 6s.

'A story of exquisite tenderness, of most delicate fancy.'—*Pall Mall Gazette.*
'It contains many of the finer characteristics of her best work.'—*Scotsman.*
'It is little short of sacrilege on the part of a reviewer to attempt to sketch its outlines or analyse its peculiar charm.'—*Spectator.*

Messrs. Methuen's List

W. E. Norris. MATTHEW AUSTIN. By W. E. NORRIS, Author of 'Mademoiselle de Mersac,' etc. *Fourth Edition. Crown 8vo.* 6s.

"An intellectually satisfactory and morally bracing novel.'—*Daily Telegraph.*

W. E. Norris. HIS GRACE. By W. E. NORRIS. *Third Edition. Crown 8vo.* 6s.

'Mr. Norris has drawn a really fine character in the Duke of Hurstbourne, at once unconventional and very true to the conventionalities of life.'—*Athenæum.*

W. E. Norris. THE DESPOTIC LADY AND OTHERS. By W. E. NORRIS. *Crown 8vo.* 6s.

'A budget of good fiction of which no one will tire.'—*Scotsman.*

W. E. Norris. CLARISSA FURIOSA. By W. E. NORRIS, *Crown 8vo.* 6s.

'As a story it is admirable, as a *jeu d'esprit* it is capital, as a lay sermon studded with gems of wit and wisdom it is a model.'—*The World.*

W. Clark Russell. MY DANISH SWEETHEART. By W. CLARK RUSSELL, Author of 'The Wreck of the Grosvenor,' etc. *Illustrated. Fourth Edition. Crown 8vo.* 6s.

Robert Barr. THE MUTABLE MANY. By ROBERT BARR, Author of 'In the Midst of Alarms,' 'A Woman Intervenes,' etc. *Second Edition. Crown 8vo.* 6s.

'Very much the best novel that Mr. Barr has yet given us. There is much insight in it, much acute and delicate appreciation of the finer shades of character and much excellent humour.'—*Daily Chronicle.*
'An excellent story. It contains several excellently studied characters, and is filled with lifelike pictures of modern life.'—*Glasgow Herald.*

Robert Barr. IN THE MIDST OF ALARMS. By ROBERT BARR. *Third Edition. Crown 8vo.* 6s.

'A book which has abundantly satisfied us by its capital humour.'—*Daily Chronicle.*
'Mr. Barr has achieved a triumph whereof he has every reason to be proud.'—*Pall Mall Gazette.*

J. Maclaren Cobban. THE KING OF ANDAMAN: A Saviour of Society. By J. MACLAREN COBBAN. *Crown 8vo.* 6s.

'An unquestionably interesting book. It contains one character, at least, who has in him the root of immortality, and the book itself is ever exhaling the sweet savour of the unexpected.'—*Pall Mall Gazette.*

J. Maclaren Cobban. WILT THOU HAVE THIS WOMAN? By J. M. COBBAN, Author of 'The King of Andaman.' *Crown 8vo.* 6s.

MESSRS. METHUEN'S LIST

Robert Hichens. BYEWAYS. By ROBERT HICHENS. Author of 'Flames,' etc. *Crown 8vo.* 6s.

'A very high artistic instinct and striking command of language raise Mr. Hichens' work far above the ruck.'—*Pall Mall Gazette.*
'The work is undeniably that of a man of striking imagination and no less striking powers of expression.'—*Daily News.*

Percy White. A PASSIONATE PILGRIM. By PERCY WHITE, Author of 'Mr. Bailey-Martin.' *Crown 8vo.* 6s.

'A work which it is not hyperbole to describe as of rare excellence.'—*Pall Mall Gazette.*
'The clever book of a shrewd and clever author.'—*Athenæum.*
'Mr. Percy White's strong point is analysis, and he has shown himself, before now, capable of building up a good book upon that foundation.'—*Standard.*

W. Pett Ridge. SECRETARY TO BAYNE, M.P. By W. PETT RIDGE. *Crown 8vo.* 6s.

'Sparkling, vivacious, adventurous.—*St. James's Gazette.*
'Ingenious, amusing, and especially smart.'—*World.*
'The dialogue is invariably alert and highly diverting.'—*Spectator.*

J. S. Fletcher. THE BUILDERS. By J. S. FLETCHER, Author of 'When Charles I. was King.' *Second Edition. Crown 8vo.* 6s.

'Replete with delightful descriptions.'—*Vanity Fair.*
'The background of country life has never, perhaps, been sketched more realistically.' —*World.*

Andrew Balfour. BY STROKE OF SWORD. By ANDREW BALFOUR. Illustrated by W. CUBITT COOKE. *Fourth Edition. Crown 8vo.* 6s.

'A banquet of good things.'—*Academy.*
'A recital of thrilling interest, told with unflagging vigour.'—*Globe*
'An unusually excellent example of a semi-historic romance.'—*World.*
'Manly, healthy, and patriotic.'—*Glasgow Herald.*

I. Hooper. THE SINGER OF MARLY. By I. HOOPER. Illustrated by W. CUBITT COOKE. *Crown 8vo.* 6s.

'Its scenes are drawn in vivid colours, and the characters are all picturesque.'— *Scotsman.*
'A novel as vigorous as it is charming.'—*Literary World.*

M. C. Balfour. THE FALL OF THE SPARROW. By M. C. BALFOUR. *Crown 8vo.* 6s.

'A powerful novel.'—*Daily Telegraph.*
'It is unusually powerful, and the characterization is uncommonly good.'—*World.*
'It is a well-knit, carefully-wrought story.'—*Academy.*

H. Morrah. A SERIOUS COMEDY. By HERBERT MORRAH. *Crown 8vo.* 6s.

H. Morrah. THE FAITHFUL CITY. By HERBERT MORRAH, Author of 'A Serious Comedy.' *Crown 8vo.* 6s.

L. B. Walford. SUCCESSORS TO THE TITLE. By Mrs. WALFORD, Author of 'Mr. Smith,' etc. *Second Edition. Crown 8vo.* 6s.

Mary Gaunt. KIRKHAM'S FIND. By MARY GAUNT, Author of 'The Moving Finger.' *Crown 8vo.* 6s.

'A really charming novel.'—*Standard.*
'A capital book, in which will be found lively humour, penetrating insight, and the sweet savour of a thoroughly healthy moral.'—*Speaker.*

M. M. Dowie. GALLIA. By MÉNIE MURIEL DOWIE, Author of 'A Girl in the Carpathians.' *Third Edition. Crown 8vo.* 6s.

'The style is generally admirable, the dialogue not seldom brilliant, the situations surprising in their freshness and originality, while the characters live and move, and the story itself is readable from title-page to colophon.'—*Saturday Review.*

J. A. Barry. IN THE GREAT DEEP. By J. A. BARRY. Author of 'Steve Brown's Bunyip.' *Crown 8vo.* 6s.

'A collection of really admirable short stories of the sea, very simply told, and placed before the reader in pithy and telling English.'—*Westminster Gazette.*

J. B. Burton. IN THE DAY OF ADVERSITY. By J. BLOUNDELLE-BURTON.' *Second Edition. Crown 8vo.* 6s.

'Unusually interesting and full of highly dramatic situations. —*Guardian.*

J. B. Burton. DENOUNCED. By J. BLOUNDELLE-BURTON. *Second Edition. Crown 8vo.* 6s.

'The plot is an original one, and the local colouring is laid on with a delicacy and an accuracy of detail which denote the true artist.'—*Broad Arrow.*

J. B. Burton. THE CLASH OF ARMS. By J. BLOUNDELLE-BURTON, Author of 'In the Day of Adversity.' *Second Edition. Crown 8vo.* 6s.

'A brave story—brave in deed, brave in word, brave in thought.'—*St. James's Gazette.*
'A fine, manly, spirited piece of work.'—*World.*

W. C. Scully. THE WHITE HECATOMB. By W. C. SCULLY, Author of 'Kafir Stories.' *Crown 8vo.* 6s.

'It reveals a marvellously intimate understanding of the Kaffir mind, allied with literary gifts of no mean order.'—*African Critic.*

Julian Corbett. A BUSINESS IN GREAT WATERS. By JULIAN CORBETT. *Second Edition. Crown 8vo.* 6s.

'Mr. Corbett writes with immense spirit. The salt of the ocean is in it, and the right heroic ring resounds through its gallant adventures.'—*Speaker*

L. Cope Cornford. CAPTAIN JACOBUS: A ROMANCE OF THE ROAD. By L. COPE CORNFORD. Illustrated. *Crown 8vo.* 6s.

'An exceptionally good story of adventure and character.'—*World.*

L. Daintrey. THE KING OF ALBERIA. A Romance of the Balkans. By LAURA DAINTREY. *Crown 8vo.* 6s.

M. A. Owen. THE DAUGHTER OF ALOUETTE. By MARY A. OWEN. *Crown 8vo.* 6s.

Messrs. Methuen's List

Mrs. Pinsent. CHILDREN OF THIS WORLD. By ELLEN F. PINSENT, Author of 'Jenny's Case.' *Crown 8vo.* 6s.

G. Manville Fenn. AN ELECTRIC SPARK. By G. MANVILLE FENN, Author of 'The Vicar's Wife,' 'A Double Knot,' etc. *Second Edition. Crown 8vo.* 6s.

L. S. McChesney. UNDER SHADOW OF THE MISSION. By L. S. MCCHESNEY. *Crown 8vo.* 6s.

'Those whose minds are open to the finer issues of life, who can appreciate graceful thought and refined expression of it, from them this volume will receive a welcome as enthusiastic as it will be based on critical knowledge.'—*Church Times.*

J. F. Brewer. THE SPECULATORS. By J. F. BREWER. *Second Edition. Crown 8vo.* 6s.

Ronald Ross. THE SPIRIT OF STORM. By RONALD ROSS, Author of 'The Child of Ocean.' *Crown 8vo.* 6s.

C. P. Wolley. THE QUEENSBERRY CUP. A Tale of Adventure. By CLIVE P. LLEY. *Illustrated. Crown 8vo.* 6s.

T. L. Paton. A HOME IN INVERESK. By T. L. PATON. *Crown 8vo.* 6s.

John Davidson. MISS ARMSTRONG'S AND OTHER CIRCUMSTANCES. By JOHN DAVIDSON. *Crown 8vo.* 6s.

H. Johnston. DR. CONGALTON'S LEGACY. By HENRY JOHNSTON. *Crown 8vo.* 6s.

R. Pryce. TIME AND THE WOMAN. By RICHARD PRYCE. *Second Edition. Crown 8vo.* 6s.

Mrs. Watson. THIS MAN'S DOMINION. By the Author of 'A High Little World.' *Second Edition. Crown 8vo.* 6s.

Marriott Watson. DIOGENES OF LONDON. By H. B. MARRIOTT WATSON. *Crown 8vo. Buckram.* 6s.

M. Gilchrist. THE STONE DRAGON. By MURRAY GILCHRIST. *Crown 8vo. Buckram.* 6s.

E. Dickinson. A VICAR'S WIFE. By EVELYN DICKINSON. *Crown 8vo.* 6s.

E. M. Gray. ELSA. By E. M'QUEEN GRAY. *Crown 8vo.* 6s.

MESSRS. METHUEN'S LIST   33

THREE-AND-SIXPENNY NOVELS
Crown 8vo.

DERRICK VAUGHAN, NOVELIST. By EDNA LYALL.
MARGERY OF QUETHER. By S. BARING GOULD.
JACQUETTA. By S. BARING GOULD.
SUBJECT TO VANITY. By MARGARET BENSON.
THE SIGN OF THE SPIDER. By BERTRAM MITFORD.
THE MOVING FINGER. By MARY GAUNT.
JACO TRELOAR. By J. H. PEARCE.
THE DANCE OF THE HOURS. By 'VERA.'
A WOMAN OF FORTY. By ESMÉ STUART.
A CUMBERER OF THE GROUND. By CONSTANCE SMITH.
THE SIN OF ANGELS. By EVELYN DICKINSON.
AUT DIABOLUS AUT NIHIL. By X. L.
THE COMING OF CUCULAIN. By STANDISH O'GRADY.
THE GODS GIVE MY DONKEY WINGS. By ANGUS EVAN ABBOTT.
THE STAR GAZERS. By G. MANVILLE FENN.
THE POISON OF ASPS. By R. ORTON PROWSE.
THE QUIET MRS. FLEMING. By R. PRYCE.
DISENCHANTMENT. By F. MABEL ROBINSON.
THE SQUIRE OF WANDALES. By A. SHIELD.
A REVEREND GENTLEMAN. By J. M. COBBAN.
A DEPLORABLE AFFAIR. By W. E. NORRIS.
A CAVALIER'S LADYE. By Mrs. DICKER.
THE PRODIGALS. By Mrs. OLIPHANT.
THE SUPPLANTER. By P. NEUMANN.
A MAN WITH BLACK EYELASHES. By H. A. KENNEDY.
A HANDFUL OF EXOTICS. By S. GORDON.
AN ODD EXPERIMENT. By HANNAH LYNCH.
SCOTTISH BORDER LIFE. By JAMES C. DIBDIN.

HALF-CROWN NOVELS
A Series of Novels by popular Authors.

HOVENDEN, V.C. By F. MABEL ROBINSON.
THE PLAN OF CAMPAIGN. By F. MABEL ROBINSON.
MR. BUTLER'S WARD. By F. MABEL ROBINSON.
ELI'S CHILDREN. By G. MANVILLE FENN.
A DOUBLE KNOT. By G. MANVILLE FENN.
DISARMED. By M. BETHAM EDWARDS.
A MARRIAGE AT SEA. By W. CLARK RUSSELL.
IN TENT AND BUNGALOW. By the Author of 'Indian Idylls.'

MY STEWARDSHIP. By E. M'QUEEN GRAY.
JACK'S FATHER. By W. E. NORRIS.
JIM B.
A LOST ILLUSION. By LESLIE KEITH.

Lynn Linton. THE TRUE HISTORY OF JOSHUA DAVIDSON, Christian and Communist. By E. LYNN LINTON. *Eleventh Edition. Post 8vo.* 1s.

Books for Boys and Girls

A Series of Books by well-known Authors, well illustrated.

THREE-AND-SIXPENCE EACH

THE ICELANDER'S SWORD. By S. BARING GOULD.
TWO LITTLE CHILDREN AND CHING. By EDITH E. CUTHELL.
TODDLEBEN'S HERO. By M. M. BLAKE.
ONLY A GUARD-ROOM DOG. By EDITH E. CUTHELL.
THE DOCTOR OF THE JULIET. By HARRY COLLINGWOOD.
MASTER ROCKAFELLAR'S VOYAGE. By W. CLARK RUSSELL.
SYD BELTON: Or, The Boy who would not go to Sea. By G. MANVILLE FENN.
THE WALLYPUG IN LONDON. By G. E. FARROW.

The Peacock Library

A Series of Books for Girls by well-known Authors, handsomely bound in blue and silver, and well illustrated.

THREE-AND-SIXPENCE EACH

A PINCH OF EXPERIENCE. By L. B. WALFORD.
THE RED GRANGE. By Mrs. MOLESWORTH.
THE SECRET OF MADAME DE MONLUC. By the Author of 'Mdle Mori.'
DUMPS. By Mrs. PARR, Author of 'Adam and Eve.'
OUT OF THE FASHION. By L. T. MEADE.
A GIRL OF THE PEOPLE. By L. T. MEADE.
HEPSY GIPSY. By L. T. MEADE. 2s. 6d.
THE HONOURABLE MISS. By L. T. MEADE.
MY LAND OF BEULAH. By Mrs. LEITH ADAMS.

MESSRS. METHUEN'S LIST 35

University Extension Series

A series of books on historical, literary, and scientific subjects, suitable for extension students and home-reading circles. Each volume is complete in itself, and the subjects are treated by competent writers in a broad and philosophic spirit.

Edited by J. E. SYMES, M.A.,
Principal of University College, Nottingham.
Crown 8vo. Price (with some exceptions) 2s. 6d.
The following volumes are ready :—

THE INDUSTRIAL HISTORY OF ENGLAND. By H. DE B. GIBBINS, D.Litt., M.A., late Scholar of Wadham College, Oxon., Cobden Prizeman. *Fifth Edition, Revised. With Maps and Plans.* 3s.
'A compact and clear story of our industrial development. A study of this concise but luminous book cannot fail to give the reader a clear insight into the principal phenomena of our industrial history. The editor and publishers are to be congratulated on this first volume of their venture, and we shall look with expectant interest for the succeeding volumes of the series.'—*University Extension Journal.*

A HISTORY OF ENGLISH POLITICAL ECONOMY. By L. L. PRICE, M.A., Fellow of Oriel College, Oxon. *Second Edition.*

PROBLEMS OF POVERTY: An Inquiry into the Industrial Conditions of the Poor. By J. A. HOBSON, M.A. *Third Edition.*

VICTORIAN POETS. By A. SHARP.

THE FRENCH REVOLUTION. By J. E. SYMES, M.A.

PSYCHOLOGY. By F. S. GRANGER, M.A. *Second Edition.*

THE EVOLUTION OF PLANT LIFE: Lower Forms. By G. MASSEE. *With Illustrations.*

AIR AND WATER. By V. B. LEWES, M.A. *Illustrated.*

THE CHEMISTRY OF LIFE AND HEALTH. By C. W. KIMMINS, M.A. *Illustrated.*

THE MECHANICS OF DAILY LIFE. By V. P. SELLS, M.A. *Illustrated.*

ENGLISH SOCIAL REFORMERS. By H. DE B. GIBBINS, D.Litt., M.A.

ENGLISH TRADE AND FINANCE IN THE SEVENTEENTH CENTURY. By W. A. S. HEWINS, B.A.

THE CHEMISTRY OF FIRE. The Elementary Principles of Chemistry. By M. M. PATTISON MUIR, M.A. *Illustrated.*

A TEXT-BOOK OF AGRICULTURAL BOTANY. By M. C. POTTER, M.A., F.L.S. *Illustrated.* 3s. 6d.

THE VAULT OF HEAVEN. A Popular Introduction to Astronomy. By R. A. GREGORY. *With numerous Illustrations.*

METEOROLOGY. The Elements of Weather and Climate. By H. N. DICKSON, F.R.S.E., F.R. Met. Soc. *Illustrated.*

A MANUAL OF ELECTRICAL SCIENCE. By GEORGE J. BURCH, M.A. *With numerous Illustrations.* 3s.

THE EARTH. An Introduction to Physiography. By EVAN SMALL, M.A. *Illustrated.*

INSECT LIFE. By F. W. THEOBALD, M.A. *Illustrated.*

ENGLISH POETRY FROM BLAKE TO BROWNING. By W. M. DIXON, M.A.

ENGLISH LOCAL GOVERNMENT. By E. JENKS, M.A., Professor of Law at University College, Liverpool.

THE GREEK VIEW OF LIFE. By G. L. DICKINSON, Fellow of King's College, Cambridge. *Second Edition.*

Social Questions of To-day

Edited by H. DE B. GIBBINS, D.Litt., M.A.

Crown 8vo. 2s. 6d.

A series of volumes upon those topics of social, economic, and industrial interest that are at the present moment foremost in the public mind. Each volume of the series is written by an author who is an acknowledged authority upon the subject with which he deals.

The following Volumes of the Series are ready:—

TRADE UNIONISM—NEW AND OLD. By G. HOWELL. *Second Edition.*

THE CO-OPERATIVE MOVEMENT TO-DAY. By G. J. HOLYOAKE, *Second Edition.*

MUTUAL THRIFT. By Rev. J. FROME WILKINSON, M.A.

PROBLEMS OF POVERTY. By J. A. HOBSON, M.A. *Third Edition.*

THE COMMERCE OF NATIONS. By C. F. BASTABLE, M.A., Professor of Economics at Trinity College, Dublin.

THE ALIEN INVASION. By W. H. WILKINS, B.A.

THE RURAL EXODUS. By P. ANDERSON GRAHAM.

LAND NATIONALIZATION. By HAROLD COX, B.A.

A SHORTER WORKING DAY. By H. DE B. GIBBINS, D.Litt., M.A., and R. A. HADFIELD, of the Hecla Works, Sheffield.

BACK TO THE LAND: An Inquiry into the Cure for Rural Depopulation. By H. E. MOORE.

TRUSTS, POOLS AND CORNERS. By J. STEPHEN JEANS.

THE FACTORY SYSTEM. By R. W. COOKE-TAYLOR.

THE STATE AND ITS CHILDREN. By GERTRUDE TUCKWELL.

MESSRS. METHUEN'S LIST 37

WOMEN'S WORK. By LADY DILKE, Miss BULLEY, and Miss WHITLEY.

MUNICIPALITIES AT WORK. The Municipal Policy of Six Great Towns, and its Influence on their Social Welfare. By FREDERICK DOLMAN.

SOCIALISM AND MODERN THOUGHT. By M. KAUFMANN.

THE HOUSING OF THE WORKING CLASSES. By E. BOWMAKER.

MODERN CIVILIZATION IN SOME OF ITS ECONOMIC ASPECTS. By W. CUNNINGHAM, D.D., Fellow of Trinity College, Cambridge.

THE PROBLEM OF THE UNEMPLOYED. By J. A. HOBSON, B.A.,

LIFE IN WEST LONDON. By ARTHUR SHERWELL, M.A. *Second Edition*.

RAILWAY NATIONALIZATION. By CLEMENT EDWARDS.

Classical Translations

Edited by H. F. FOX, M.A., Fellow and Tutor of Brasenose College, Oxford.

ÆSCHYLUS—Agamemnon, Chöephoroe, Eumenides. Translated by LEWIS CAMPBELL, LL.D., late Professor of Greek at St. Andrews, 5s.

CICERO—De Oratore I. Translated by E. N. P. MOOR, M.A. 3s. 6d.

CICERO — Select Orations (Pro Milone, Pro Murena, Philippic II., In Catilinam). Translated by H. E. D. BLAKISTON, M.A., Fellow and Tutor of Trinity College, Oxford. 5s.

CICERO—De Natura Deorum. Translated by F. BROOKS, M.A., late Scholar of Balliol College, Oxford. 3s. 6d.

LUCIAN—Six Dialogues (Nigrinus, Icaro-Menippus, The Cock, The Ship, The Parasite, The Lover of Falsehood). Translated by S. T. IRWIN, M.A., Assistant Master at Clifton ; late Scholar of Exeter College, Oxford. 3s. 6d.

SOPHOCLES—Electra and Ajax. Translated by E. D. A. MORSHEAD, M.A., Assistant Master at Winchester. 2s. 6d.

TACITUS—Agricola and Germania. Translated by R. B. TOWNSHEND, late Scholar of Trinity College, Cambridge. 2s. 6d.

Educational Books

CLASSICAL

PLAUTI BACCHIDES. Edited with Introduction, Commentary, and Critical Notes by J. M'COSH, M.A. *Fcap. 4to.* 12s. 6d.
'The notes are copious, and contain a great deal of information that is good and useful.'—*Classical Review*.

TACITI AGRICOLI. With Introduction, Notes, Map, etc. By R. F. DAVIS, M.A., Assistant Master at Weymouth College. *Crown 8vo.* 2s.

TACITI GERMANIA. By the same Editor. *Crown 8vo.* 2s.

HERODOTUS : EASY SELECTIONS. With Vocabulary. By A. C. LIDDELL, M.A. *Fcap. 8vo.* 1s. 6d.

SELECTIONS FROM THE ODYSSEY. By E. D. STONE, M.A., late Assistant Master at Eton. *Fcap. 8vo.* 1s. 6d.

PLAUTUS: THE CAPTIVI. Adapted for Lower Forms by J. H. FRESSE, M.A., late Fellow of St. John's, Cambridge. 1s. 6d.

DEMOSTHENES AGAINST CONON AND CALLICLES. Edited with Notes and Vocabulary, by F. DARWIN SWIFT, M.A., formerly Scholar of Queen's College, Oxford. *Fcap. 8vo.* 2s.

EXERCISES ON LATIN ACCIDENCE. By S. E. WINBOLT, Assistant Master at Christ's Hospital. *Crown 8vo.* 1s. 6d.

An elementary book adapted for Lower Forms to accompany the shorter Latin primer.
'Skilfully arranged.'—*Glasgow Herald.*
'Accurate and well arranged.'—*Athenæum.*

NOTES ON GREEK AND LATIN SYNTAX. By G. BUCKLAND GREEN, M.A., Assistant Master at Edinburgh Academy, late Fellow of St. John's College, Oxon. *Crown 8vo.* 2s. 6d.

Notes and explanations on the chief difficulties of Greek and Latin Syntax, with numerous passages for exercise.
'Supplies a gap in educational literature.'—*Glasgow Herald.*

GERMAN

A COMPANION GERMAN GRAMMAR. By H. DE B. GIBBINS, D.Litt., M.A., Assistant Master at Nottingham High School. *Crown 8vo.* 1s. 6d.

GERMAN PASSAGES FOR UNSEEN TRANSLATION. By E. M'QUEEN GRAY. *Crown 8vo.* 2s. 6d.

SCIENCE

THE WORLD OF SCIENCE. Including Chemistry, Heat, Light, Sound, Magnetism, Electricity, Botany, Zoology, Physiology, Astronomy, and Geology. By R. ELLIOTT STEEL, M.A., F.C.S. 147 Illustrations. *Second Edition. Crown 8vo.* 2s. 6d.

ELEMENTARY LIGHT. By R. E. STEEL. With numerous Illustrations. *Crown 8vo.* 4s. 6d.

ENGLISH

ENGLISH RECORDS. A Companion to the History of England. By H. E. MALDEN, M.A. *Crown 8vo.* 3s. 6d.

A book which aims at concentrating information upon dates, genealogy, officials, constitutional documents, etc., which is usually found scattered in different volumes.

THE ENGLISH CITIZEN: HIS RIGHTS AND DUTIES. By H. E. MALDEN, M.A. 1s. 6d.

A DIGEST OF DEDUCTIVE LOGIC. By JOHNSON BARKER, B.A. *Crown 8vo.* 2s. 6d.

MESSRS. METHUEN'S LIST

METHUEN'S COMMERCIAL SERIES

Edited by H. DE B. GIBBINS, D.Litt., M.A.

BRITISH COMMERCE AND COLONIES FROM ELIZABETH TO VICTORIA. By H. DE B. GIBBINS, D.Litt., M.A. 2s. *Second Edition.*
COMMERCIAL EXAMINATION PAPERS. By H. DE B. GIBBINS, D.Litt., M.A., 1s. 6d.
THE ECONOMICS OF COMMERCE. By H. DE B. GIBBINS, D.Litt., M.A. 1s. 6d.
FRENCH COMMERCIAL CORRESPONDENCE. By S. E. BALLY, Modern Language Master at the Manchester Grammar School. 2s. *Second Edition.*
GERMAN COMMERCIAL CORRESPONDENCE. By S. E. BALLY, 2s. 6d.
A FRENCH COMMERCIAL READER. By S. E. BALLY. 2s.
COMMERCIAL GEOGRAPHY, with special reference to Trade Routes, New Markets, and Manufacturing Districts. By L. W. LYDE, M.A., of the Academy, Glasgow. 2s. *Second Edition.*
A PRIMER OF BUSINESS. By S. JACKSON, M.A. 1s. 6d.
COMMERCIAL ARITHMETIC. By F. G. TAYLOR, M.A. 1s. 6d.
PRÉCIS WRITING AND OFFICE CORRESPONDENCE. By E. E. WHITFIELD, M.A. 2s.

WORKS BY A. M. M. STEDMAN, M.A.

INITIA LATINA: Easy Lessons on Elementary Accidence. *Second Edition. Fcap. 8vo.* 1s.
FIRST LATIN LESSONS. *Fourth Edition. Crown 8vo.* 2s.
FIRST LATIN READER. With Notes adapted to the Shorter Latin Primer and Vocabulary. *Fourth Edition revised.* 18mo. 1s. 6d.
EASY SELECTIONS FROM CAESAR. Part I. The Helvetian War. 18mo. 1s.
EASY SELECTIONS FROM LIVY. Part I. The Kings of Rome. 18mo. 1s. 6d.
EASY LATIN PASSAGES FOR UNSEEN TRANSLATION. *Fifth Edition. Fcap. 8vo.* 1s. 6d.
EXEMPLA LATINA. First Lessons in Latin Accidence. With Vocabulary. *Crown 8vo.* 1s.
EASY LATIN EXERCISES ON THE SYNTAX OF THE SHORTER AND REVISED LATIN PRIMER. With Vocabulary. *Seventh and cheaper Edition re-written. Crown 8vo.* 1s. 6d. Issued with the consent of Dr. Kennedy.
THE LATIN COMPOUND SENTENCE: Rules and Exercises. *Crown 8vo.* 1s. 6d. With Vocabulary. 2s.
NOTANDA QUAEDAM: Miscellaneous Latin Exercises on Common Rules and Idioms. *Third Edition. Fcap. 8vo.* 1s. 6d. With Vocabulary. 2s.
LATIN VOCABULARIES FOR REPETITION: Arranged according to Subjects. *Sixth Edition. Fcap. 8vo.* 1s. 6d.

40 MESSRS. METHUEN'S LIST

A VOCABULARY OF LATIN IDIOMS AND PHRASES. 18mo. *Second Edition.* 1s.

STEPS TO GREEK. 18mo. 1s.

EASY GREEK PASSAGES FOR UNSEEN TRANSLATION. *Third Edition revised.* Fcap. 8vo. 1s. 6d.

GREEK VOCABULARIES FOR REPETITION. Arranged according to Subjects. *Second Edition.* Fcap. 8vo. 1s. 6d.

GREEK TESTAMENT SELECTIONS. For the use of Schools. *Third Edition.* With Introduction, Notes, and Vocabulary. Fcap. 8vo. 2s. 6d.

STEPS TO FRENCH. *Second Edition.* 18mo. 8d.

FIRST FRENCH LESSONS. *Second Edition.* Crown 8vo. 1s.

EASY FRENCH PASSAGES FOR UNSEEN TRANSLATION. *Third Edition revised.* Fcap. 8vo. 1s. 6d.

EASY FRENCH EXERCISES ON ELEMENTARY SYNTAX. With Vocabulary. Crown 8vo. 2s. 6d.

FRENCH VOCABULARIES FOR REPETITION : Arranged according to Subjects. *Fifth Edition.* Fcap. 8vo. 1s.

SCHOOL EXAMINATION SERIES

EDITED BY A. M. M. STEDMAN, M.A. *Crown 8vo. 2s. 6d.*

FRENCH EXAMINATION PAPERS IN MISCELLANEOUS GRAMMAR AND IDIOMS. By A. M. M. STEDMAN, M.A. *Ninth Edition.*
A KEY, issued to Tutors and Private Students only, to be had on application to the Publishers. *Fourth Edition. Crown 8vo. 6s. net.*

LATIN EXAMINATION PAPERS IN MISCELLANEOUS GRAMMAR AND IDIOMS. By A. M. M. STEDMAN, M.A. *Eighth Edition.*
KEY (*Third Edition*) issued as above. 6s. net.

GREEK EXAMINATION PAPERS IN MISCELLANEOUS GRAMMAR AND IDIOMS. By A. M. M. STEDMAN, M.A. *Fifth Edition.*
KEY (*Second Edition*) issued as above. 6s. net.

GERMAN EXAMINATION PAPERS IN MISCELLANEOUS GRAMMAR AND IDIOMS. By R. J. MORICH, Manchester. *Fifth Edition.*
KEY (*Second Edition*) issued as above. 6s. net.

HISTORY AND GEOGRAPHY EXAMINATION PAPERS. By C. H. SPENCE, M.A., Clifton College.

SCIENCE EXAMINATION PAPERS. By R. E. STEEL, M.A., F.C.S., Chief Natural Science Master, Bradford Grammar School. *In two vols.* Part I. Chemistry ; Part II. Physics.

GENERAL KNOWLEDGE EXAMINATION PAPERS. By A. M. M. STEDMAN, M.A. *Third Edition.*
KEY (*Second Edition*) issued as above. 7s. net.

www.ingramcontent.com/pod-product-compliance
Lightning Source LLC
Chambersburg PA
CBHW070529090426
42735CB00013B/2914